Reading and Speaking
Foreign Languages

Reading and Speaking Foreign Languages

By H. R. HUSE

THE UNIVERSITY OF NORTH CAROLINA PRESS

Chapel Hill

COPYRIGHT, 1945, BY

The University of North Carolina Press

Van Rees Press · New York · PJ

PREFACE

RECENTLY there has been a renewed interest in language teaching. The new internationalism, the movement for Basic English, the Army experiments in teaching foreign languages, and the emphasis on area studies have all led to much popular writing and to many sensational announcements.

Unfortunately, language is one of the subjects that invite the most absolute and most irresponsible of convictions. Everyone has his views: small children can spot at once anyone who "talks funny." For some affected people, an Oxford accent is an unquestionable criterion of distinction: it silences argument.

Most of those who, like myself, took some part in the Army ASTP program had an extremely limited experience in one unit. If they reached no unusual conclusions, as a rule they said nothing. Others, promoting something, or with startling and optimistic discoveries, had almost a monopoly of the publicity. Some of the most unfortunate articles were written by college presidents who had heard from others in their institutions about the great success and the sudden and triumphant solution of an old problem. Newspapers told how students, starting from scratch, learned to speak the most difficult tongues "just like a native" in a few weeks, an attainment that abundant, every-day experience in America shows to be impossible for most foreigners even after forty or fifty years. Additional time and a period of less universal dementia are needed to evaluate accurately the ASTP experiments.

Still the need for some reform in language instruction is urgent. The unexpected flood of students who came to high school and college long after the traditional curriculum was established overwhelmed the more serious and difficult subjects. And in many secondary schools and in some colleges, all language study has been threatened with extinction.

I should like to see language study saved, and that is one of the reasons for this book. It can be saved when the aims are limited for each type of course, when they are clearly announced, and when the particular methods are related to those aims. A number of developments have made possible a remarkable progress in the presentation of linguistic material for memorization.

The first draft of this book was written some time ago and a few of the notes I had taken have been lost. If, in one or two cases, I cannot acknowledge all the debt to others I have incurred, I trust the injustice will be attributed to accident and not to intention.

H. R. HUSE

Chapel Hill, N. C., June, 1945.

CONTENTS

Preface   v

Part I
A CRITICISM OF FOREIGN LANGUAGE INSTRUCTION

I. The Talent for Speaking   3
II. The Effects of Bilingualism   14
III. The Present Disorder   26

Part II
A DEFENSE OF FOREIGN LANGUAGE STUDY

IV. Why Study a Foreign Language?   45

Part III
METHODS, WORD COUNTS, TEXTBOOKS

V. The Battle of the Methods   63
VI. Word Counts and Units of Expression   84
VII. Textbooks in Foreign Languages   95

Part IV
SUGGESTIONS FOR A SCIENTIFIC METHOD OF LANGUAGE TEACHING

VIII. A Plan for Teaching How to Read   103
Notes   121
Bibliography   124
Index   126

Part One

A CRITICISM OF FOREIGN LANGUAGE INSTRUCTION

I

The Talent for Speaking

FACILITY IN SPEECH is almost unrelated to serious intellectual powers. Women are notoriously more voluble than men. Girls usually learn to speak more quickly than boys and speak more clearly and with less hesitation. Among boys there is a greater proportion of stammerers and of those with other speech defects.[1] This difference has been universally noted and incorporated in the proverbs of nearly all countries. *"Où femme il y a, silence n'y a." "Due donne e un'oca fanno una fiera."* "The North Sea will sooner be found wanting in water than a woman at a loss for a word."[2]

Thought is usually hostile to fluency. Politicians and salesmen are generally more fluent than philosophers and scientists. As Swift says, "The common fluency of speech in many men and most women is owing to the scarcity of matter and scarcity of words; for whoever is a master of language and with a mind full of ideas will be apt in speaking to hesitate upon the choice of both: whereas common speakers have only one set of ideas and one set of words to clothe them in; and these are always ready at the mouth. So people come faster out of a church when it is almost empty than when a crowd is at the door."

The facility of some voluble women—the *"belles langagières"* to whom Villon refers—is due to the fact that they confine themselves to the central field of language and their speech is less troubled by self-criticism, fine distinctions, thought, and objectivity.

AUTOMATIC SPEECH

The reasons for facility of speech in many relatively thoughtless persons are not difficult to find. Speech is easiest and most fluent when it is automatic, and it is often automatic in everyone. We can talk while devoting most of our attention to something else. The more conventional and unreflective the phrases are, the smoother and more rapid the utterance. Such designations as "the land of the free and the home of the brave" almost speak themselves. Whole sentences are often merely expanded words and come to the tongue as automatically as exclamations ("Ouch!" "Fire!") or symbols for simple objects in common use.

It has been claimed that language sometimes takes the place of thought, as in the speeches of many popular orators who have only the vaguest idea of what they are going to say before starting. One word suggests another, the end of one sentence produces the beginning of the next, and a series of remarks follows, like a string of overlapping cards that fall one after the other when the first is turned.

DISTRIBUTION OF LINGUISTIC TALENT

Especially in speaking a foreign tongue, thoughtfulness and originality are of negative value. The speaker, unless extremely proficient, must confine himself to commonplace phrases in order to avoid unidiomatic expressions.

Dr. A. F. Bronner affirms that low-grade feeble-minded persons sometimes show facility in the use of several languages.[3] Insane patients, especially in manic states, are often voluble, and those with schizophrenia frequently invent new tongues.

Common observation reveals that young children do better in picking up foreign tongues than older ones. Sailors, waiters, porters, and money-changers often display a surprising aptitude. Among peoples that have preëminence as linguists, those that stand highest in this respect are most backward in their own literature and culture. Present-day Greeks, Levantines, Syrians and Armenians are near the top of the scale in linguistic ability, whereas Americans, Englishmen, and Frenchmen (in about that order) are near the bottom, although their literatures are more highly developed. The African Bantus are reported as speaking half a dozen languages fluently.[4]

The facility of children in picking up foreign tongues is a constant source of wonder. What is more impressive than to see a little American or English child abroad rattling away in modern Greek, Chinese, or Finnish? It astounds us, like a feat of genius. But no great superiority is necessary: all average children placed in the same circumstances will do the same.

Among cultivated men there have been a few famous, practical linguists—men who have spoken or claimed to speak thirty or forty languages—but they have not been notably distinguished in other ways and, curiously, have made few contributions to the study of language. Talented linguists in the *practical* sense are rare among industrial and business leaders, scientists, philosophers, academicians, and even among Ph.D.'s in the field of language and literature. These latter are almost constantly outshone, as practical linguists, by persons of lesser education and humbler employment. The familiar idle ladies who study for twenty or thirty years and who are still hiring tutors at the age of fifty, generally cut a poor figure as linguists in comparison with less respectable and even less intelligent women in port towns.

As a matter of fact, extraordinary facility in speaking foreign tongues is found in the most unexpected places. A missionary is reported as preaching in Spanish, French, Mandarin Chinese, Japanese, Italian, and English.[5] A telephone girl in Cairo answers calls in Arabic, French, English, Italian, and Greek. A postoffice employee in Jerusalem uses all these and in addition German, Yiddish, Hebrew, Spanish, Armenian, and Turkish. For a Cairene donkey boy, according to W. H. Worrel, "life is just one language after another."[6]

Obviously a talent for speaking foreign languages is found not only in children but in adults quite undistinguished for other abilities. In government and business this fact is generally recognized.

LINGUISTIC ABILITY AND IMMATURITY

In the merely practical, narrow sense (with which this book deals largely), linguistic ability is a function of immaturity. This is almost the dominant fact in the whole situation; it must be kept in mind constantly.

On the physical side, that is, in his ability to reproduce sound, the child has a clear and understandable superiority. His habits of articulation are less firmly fixed; the paths or grooves are worn less deep. He possesses the same advantage that a boy of sixteen has over a man of forty in learning golf. There is a flexibility of the muscles that age diminishes.

Hearing, also, is more accurate in childhood. Nearly all adults who have read and studied much become visualizers; often they cannot perceive clearly the sound of a strange name without having it spelled. The child, moreover, is not confused by the capricious divisions of speech sounds into words: he hears and reproduces phrases as a whole. He depends more upon his ears than his eyes. And he profits in this respect as in others from the lack of rigidity in his habits and knowledge.

But perfection in sound reproduction, however important, is relatively a minor matter. Few adults can ever hope for it anyway. We have all seen Germans, Italians, and Frenchmen who have been in the United States for so long that they have almost forgotten their native speech and yet who do not pronounce exactly as we do. The hope of talking "just like a Frenchman" is chimerical for adults in most cases—a fact that is curiously coupled with a feeling that nothing less than perfection can satisfy. To pronounce with a truly "distinguished" accent is one thing, to "get along" is another. This last attainment should give some measure of satisfaction to sensible men; and in most languages adults can learn at least to make themselves understood.

A more serious problem is to find the words and phrases to be pronounced as best one can. And here also, curiously, a grown person cuts but a poor figure compared with a child. The adult's speech is usually halting and labored, and often comes to a complete stop. This is true of those who have studied a foreign language for years, whereas a child of five, after a few months abroad, will chatter glibly, idiomatically, and will be almost undistinguishable linguistically from other children of the same age.

Here is a mystery an understanding of which might throw light on the problem of learning to speak foreign languages and on the nature of that attainment. In simple form, the situation is this: A child whose rational faculties are undeveloped, who can concentrate only for brief moments, who scarcely reads and has little idea of how to study, nevertheless seems to make greater progress in learning a foreign language than an adult trained in memorizing and in mental work, with tutors, dictionaries, grammars, phrase books—in short, with all the apparent advantages.

THE ADVANTAGE OF IMMATURITY

The superiority of the child in the *active* use of foreign languages might seem at first sight to depend upon the relative emptiness of his head. And, as a matter of fact, his immaturity does explain his advantage. Let us consider the case of a child going to a foreign country with his father. The child has a little group of concepts with the verbal labels that go with them. His task now is to duplicate this series of symbols, an accomplishment which is easy precisely in proportion to the brevity of the list. When it *is* duplicated, his "linguistic age" (to invent a new term) and his "mental age" are in balance; that is, he never thinks of anything to say that he does not have the means to express. In an extremely hypothetical case, the vocabulary might consist of one word "papa," say, for every person wearing trousers. In that situation the child would need to duplicate only this one articulation in order to be as fluent as he was in his native tongue.

In the case of an educated adult, however, the labels, concepts, and symbols of his language represent a lifetime of study and experience. Every object he has learned to distinguish and identify has been accompanied by an articulation. Concepts and symbols are so closely bound together that almost no experience reaches consciousness except in the form of words. The distinctions between "papa," "cousin," "uncle," "citizen," "stranger," "salesman," etc., etc., are fixed in their designations. The adult can learn ten or fifty times as many linguistic units as the child and still be unable to speak easily. Why? Because there is still a disparity between his mental age and his linguistic equipment.

It is not what you *can* say that counts for fluency, but the relationship between what you *want* to say and the means you have to say it. A child never wants to express distinctions and qualifications that are not in his mind. The existence of these distinctions without complete means to express them causes the inhibitions in the adult's speech. The grown person has too many thoughts, too complicated thoughts; he lives in a world of too many differentiations. It is as if two persons started to walk in a given direction, one following the other after a long interval of time: if the direction were suddenly reversed, the one who had started first and gone farthest would have the least chance of beating the other back.

This explanation takes care of facts that everyone can observe, namely, that facility in foreign speech varies in inverse ratio to maturity, learning, and mental content. An educated adult may have a vocabulary of tens of thousands of items, a baby of one or two. It is not enough to duplicate a part of one's vocabulary in any one field; the very existence of the additional concepts and distinctions causes interference, creates inhibitions, starts the speaker on paths and into areas in which he gets lost, and destroys fluency and ease.

In acquiring a *reading* knowledge of a foreign language, the situation of an adult as compared with a child changes completely. Here the adult has an enormous advantage over the child who may not be able even to read at all.

ACTIVE COMPARED WITH PASSIVE KNOWLEDGE

There is a profound difference between an *active* (speaking) knowledge of a foreign language and a *passive* (reading) knowledge. It is the difference between recognizing the act of swimming, and swimming; the difference between knowing what a juggler is doing, and duplicating the performance.

Speech to be fluent involves a series of complicated reflexes. We spend all our lives developing the habits involved. When we see a certain object, a word comes to our mind automatically, just as we say "Ouch!" (or a more expressive variant) when we hit our fingers with a hammer. Likewise for every feeling, command, wish, or thought, a verbal expression occurs spontaneously. Speech in a foreign tongue demands changing all these infinitely complex reflexes. The more extensive and complicated they are, the more difficult is the task.

In learning to drive an automobile, a relatively simple system of reflex movements is involved. A few of these can be changed without great difficulty, just as we can make a few changes in our speech. But suppose a driver of long experience should be called upon to use a car built on an entirely different plan. Then suppose he were put on a street where traffic passed to the left, where one stopped on the green light, moved on the red, and where one was fined for not moving at least at thirty miles an hour. The best drivers under our present system would be handicapped most, those whose skill was only partly developed, less, and beginners, least of all. The parallel is not exact, but the situation is similar in the case of the linguistic reflexes necessary for speaking Chinese, say, or even French.

The question of linguistic interference belongs more

THE TALENT FOR SPEAKING 11

directly under the heading "bilingualism," but the analogy with automobile driving helps to explain what is involved. A driver of long experience might acquire an entirely new method of driving, and if he could abandon the first system entirely he might acquire a certain competence. But to use both methods simultaneously would involve (besides a possible nervous breakdown) inhibitions that lessen the skill in either system. In this case also the parallel with foreign language learning is not remote. We have all seen persons who could speak several languages badly but none well, and whose thought processes, moreover, had been clogged with words.

RANGE OF THE ABILITY

The term "speaking knowledge" is extremely vague. No one possesses it, surely, in an absolute sense. Even in the vernacular most of us are limited in the number of subjects about which we can talk intelligently. Relatively few of us know the necessary terminology of radio or television, higher mathematics, philosophy, physics, and so on. Sometimes a person may be able to discuss in a foreign language travel, school life, or social customs, but be unacquainted with the simplest terminology of the kitchen, the basement, or the automobile. The scholars of the Middle Ages, who used both Latin and their native speech, simply divided their fields of discourse. I doubt if Dante or St. Thomas could have discussed easily in Latin such matters as harness, carpentering, wine making, cooking, housekeeping, etc.—precisely the kind of practical subject with which conversational manuals deal.

Beyond a certain point, all gains made in speaking one language imply losses in the other. The foreigners who have written French or English in superior fashion are very few, and most of these have sacrificed their native tongue for the foreign. In general, only experiences that have been accompanied with a foreign language can be discussed with ease. There is almost no one who can do complicated arithmetical processes except in his native tongue. Language and experience are bound up almost inseparably.

In every consideration of speaking knowledge (aside from a kind of code or jargoning, which, however, sometimes impresses outsiders) the question of the balance between mental age and linguistic equipment comes up. All methods bump against this wall. If it were possible to reduce the mental level of students, the task would be much easier. In many cases teachers who have to face the complaint that their students do not learn to speak fluently can console themselves with the fact that the instruction has at least caused no regression in mental level, which would have made the accomplishment relatively easy.

Some persons have less difficulty, other things being equal, than others. The introverted, shy, self-examining, and self-critical have most trouble. A perfect method would have to change their natures, to make extroverts of them, at least in this respect. But to change character is a difficult task, and most introverts will remain introverts, often good thinkers, seldom good linguists.

Parents and outside observers complain of the poor results in speaking knowledge attained by the majority of foreign language students. Almost nowhere is there an understanding of what is involved. It is curious, moreover, that this ability should be rated so highly when it is found in such subordinate individuals. As Lowell has said, "The power to express the same nothing in ten different languages is something rather to be dreaded than admired. It gives a horrible advantage to dullness." But this failure, unfortunately, constitutes one clause of an indictment that has been made against *all* language study.

In most cases learning to use a language actively, that is, for speaking or writing, is difficult in proportion to age and to mental maturity. The cost in time and effort is so great that the attempt should not be made unless clear and direct gains are in sight. To enforce methods aimed at this goal as a *required* discipline in schools could easily become an abuse from which all foreign language instruction might ultimately suffer.

II

The Effects of Bilingualism

THE ATTITUDE OF small children toward language is healthy and practical. They are about the only large group of people who reveal any consistent common sense on this tricky subject. They resist instinctively any attempt to make them pronounce words or speak as a kind of accomplishment, as a means to show off.

Children seem to realize that in language all is convention; that its purpose is to express commands and emotions (mainly) in the easiest and most effective manner, and that almost nothing in speech is intrinsically good or bad, elegant or inelegant, refined or vulgar. If a child associates with children who have a southern accent, he will tend to have that accent, in spite of efforts of affected parents to make him speak Bostonese or West End. Thus Cockney children speak Cockney, South Carolinians what they hear, and so on; and in doing this they display a better understanding of what language is for than many parents (and some speech instructors) who may be confused by mistaken ambitions, inferiority complexes, and other induced maladies of the personality.

CHILDREN IN FOREIGN HOMES

Those who try to enforce unnatural linguistic conventions, instead of giving their children an advantage and a

THE EFFECTS OF BILINGUALISM

distinction, may hamper their mental development and even cause affective disturbances. Children of foreign parents in America, for example, often show mental difficulties which are due to linguistic experiences. If the parents do not speak English at all or most imperfectly, the child has to learn the foreign tongue of the parents. It is immediately useful and even necessary for him. But in absorbing so much that is foreign he differentiates himself from others in his group at school and at play; he is sometimes ashamed of his parents, and he remains or may remain a kind of foreigner in his own country. His proficiency in English rarely equals that of boys and girls from wholly American environments.

Another common situation occurs when parents, although reasonably competent in English and able to understand anything the child might say in that tongue, insist nevertheless that he should always speak to them in the foreign language. The motives behind this constraint may be quite worthy—a justified pride in race and culture, and a wish that the children should preserve this inheritance. But the restraint frequently runs counter to the instincts of the child, which direct him toward the easiest and simplest form of expression.

Up to a certain point a child does not mind learning new tongues. If he is moved from one country to another, he picks up readily the new speech and forgets the old. Some children have been obliged to learn their original language two or three times over (since they forget as quickly as they learn), but they usually submit to this necessity without complaint.

But why, the child asks, must he always speak to his mother in a foreign tongue, when nearly everyone else speaks to her in English? Like all children, he adopts and believes in the standards of the group he plays with. He doesn't want to be distinguished from others. Children are inexorable on this point, and to make them speak differently is often as cruel as sending a boy to school in a bonnet, with curls, or a béret.

Moreover, to tell about *all* experiences in a foreign tongue sometimes presents insuperable difficulties. How is a child going to describe a new game he has learned on the street, tell by a paraphrase who was "it," how many "glassies" or "taws" he won at marbles, how many "home runs" he hit? He can be silent, of course, but this involves an unnatural repression.

I have observed such a child telling his mother a story he had heard at school about Indians. The performance was painful for the teller and hearer, full of hesitation, stumbling. A new vocabulary was involved, never heard at home. *"Tu sais, maman...la maîtresse...la maîtresse nous a dit...que les* Indians (English)...*avaient...des* bows, *des* arrows...etc." This reproduction is synthetic; but the impression of painful speech was unmistakable. This boy never succeeded very well in school, not even in high school French.

FOREIGN GOVERNESSES

Another situation of less serious social importance involves the children of the rich. Fond parents, to provide talents for their offspring, impose governesses on them whose business is to talk to them in French or German. Sometimes the child learns to chatter in the foreign tongue and, if he keeps it up long enough, he may preserve this knowledge for a long time. But usually the acquirement is gained at the cost of a certain mental retardation. I have seen a young man whose governess had worked so thoroughly and long that he could address his college professors in French with ease. He seemed so advanced that there was hesitation in putting him in a class of boys not one of whom could carry on three minutes of natural conversation. But he failed, completely, flatly, even in his own estimation. Although he could talk about the weather, he could not understand the authors being read. Outside of the simplest range of discourse, he was lost. He could not explain in English, French, or by any other means at his disposal the meaning of the passages he was supposed to read. His success in other subjects, as might be supposed, was not any better. The case proves nothing; it is cited merely as an illustration of the kind of talents involved, for which some sacrifices must be made.

To interfere with a child's normal linguistic development may affect his mental life in the same way that an environment may affect his physical life. Sometimes curious and unexpected results occur. Children who have heard foreign languages as babies without ever having spoken more than a few words in them show traces of the influence in later speech. W. Stern cites the case of a child who, having lived in Silesia until the age of one and a half, was then taken to Berlin, where he never heard Silesian. At the age of five this child showed certain peculiarities of speech that could only be attributed to his experience in Silesia.[1] Another child, mentioned by Nieuwenhuis, who spoke both Dutch and English, was taken to Batavia. There his parents wanted him to learn Malay, but instead he refused to speak at all. A long treatment involving the use of a single language was necessary before he could be induced to talk again.[2]

A child will always regard any unnatural linguistic restraint as a fetter and will cast it aside if he can. His instinct is perhaps a better guide than the notions of governesses or of fashionable ladies.

BILINGUALISM AS A NATIONAL PROBLEM

In many countries the bilingual problem is of national importance. This is especially true in Switzerland, Belgium, Wales, and Quebec, and in many near- and far-Eastern areas, such as India.

The advantages of bilingualism in such countries as Switzerland are obvious. Besides the convenience in business and trade, many Swiss have open to them cultural resources of two or three great literatures. In the case of the Welsh, Bengali, and others whose native language offers only limited possibilities for cultural and scientific studies, the second language is an indispensable escape from a narrow and limiting environment. In some of these countries bilingualism must be accepted as a necessary condition of existence.

But the advantages are usually purchased at a considerable cost. As Zeller states:

The learning of his other tongue demands of the child ... such an outlay of mental activity that it will always be an exception and a proof of special language endowment when he is able, at the same time, to learn a second language without injury to his first task. The common experience can only be that which is actually found in all bilingual populations. ... Either there is produced that repulsive confounding of language, or the mother tongue is spoken only as a dialect, the foreign tongue passes for the language of the cultured, and the great mass of those who reckon themselves among these are alienated from the intellectual life and the literature of their people without, after all, in return, being able to appropriate alive the language of the foreign people as their peers. One gives up his citizenship in his own intellectual home in order, instead, to feed himself in a strange land with the fragments that he gets thrown to him with insulting condescension.[3]

LANGUAGE AND CHARACTER

The greatest possible advantages of bilingualism might be illustrated in the case of Luxemburg, whose inhabitants could be presumed to participate directly in the cultural life of two great nations. A Luxemburg author has described the situation, however, as follows:

> In obliging us from primary school on, and especially in the secondary schools to learn and to use simultaneously, day after day, two different languages, we have been accustomed to direct our attention to words and, to a less extent, to ideas. And when we spoke we expressed ourselves in one language, but we thought in another, and our consciousness, accustomed from tender childhood to this lie, did not revolt. It was as if the ray of light which shines in each of us had been broken by a prism. We became *nuancés*, capable of shining, but not of concentrating and of burning; varied colors, but no hard steel: such is our soul.[4]

A cultural infusion may become so great as to cancel one characteristic with another and leave the individual without any distinctive cultural identity.

To destroy the language of a people is to endanger its national existence, to weaken its particular character. It is through language that the spirit of a people enters into the individual. A conception of the world, a series of values, find expression normally in a people's speech.

> Each people has created for itself, little by little, a collective mentality; it has a mass of customary associations, a particular viewpoint toward things, social habits which are translated into the grammatical forms, the syntax, the values of words, the character of the metaphors. Words are the subjective repre-

sentatives of objects; they carry the idea that we have of these objects, an idea that varies from people to people; language is the mirror of the thoughts of a nation; the mentality of each race is stereotyped in its language, fixed like the image on a medal.[5]

A typical American cannot even think like a Frenchman, any more than a Frenchman can think normally like a Russian or a Chinaman.

Most writers on this subject recommend that the mother tongue be studied first. There is an intimate emotional significance in the words a child learns at home which foreign words cannot evoke. When the home language is lost or obscured, the child may become intellectually educated but emotionally sterile. Waltz writes as follows:

Apart from the overloading of the memory, it is altogether a superficial view, which can be very dangerous to the culture of the mind, if language is regarded only as an aggregate of external signs, the understanding and ready use of which is alone important. Then it would indeed be indifferent which language the child learned first, which last, and whether one alone or several together. If, on the other hand, language is the means of gradually clarifying and defining one's own inner states, if it impresses a definite national type upon the soul-life, if to the total conception of life it gives a definite coloring which enters with it and through it into the soul of the child, then it can be no indifferent matter.[6]

A further effect of bilingualism on character is due to the fact that languages tend to inhibit each other, so that by troubling both thought and speech they lessen the expressive faculty of the individual. A certain emotional instability results, it is claimed, when the mother tongue fails to provide an adequate instrument for the regulation and expression of primitive impulses. Other affective dis-

THE EFFECTS OF BILINGUALISM

turbances that have been noted in certain bilingual populations are an excess of negative attitudes, destructive urges, anti-something unions, and communal antagonisms.[7]

EFFECT ON MENTAL DEVELOPMENT

A number of investigators have studied the effect of bilingualism on mental development. Among the most important studies are those of Michael West in India, of Hughes, Saer, and Smith in Wales, and of Epstein in Switzerland. The conclusions of these investigators are not unanimous, but almost so. In varying degrees nearly all those who have studied the problem suspect bilingualism of retarding mental development, of preventing the individual from attaining his full intellectual possibilities.

For a thorough treatment of the matter, the reader should consult the authors mentioned above. A few random quotations will serve to summarize some of the findings. Smith, working in Wales, discovered that monoglot children between the ages of eight and eleven make better progress than bilingual children in the power of expression, choice of words, and accuracy of thought, and he concludes that "so far from bilingualism being an intellectual advantage, it seems to be exactly the reverse, at least under the present organization of schools in Wales." [8]

Nieuwenhuis, the Director of Public Instruction in the Dutch colonies, declares that intensive bilingualism during the first years of childhood delays the development of language and consequently exercises an unfavorable influence on the intelligence.[9] Henss comes to the same conclusion.[10] West's careful studies show that the average bilingual Bengali boy of sixteen has acquired a vocabulary barely equal to that of a normal nine- or ten-year-old monolingual English boy. The same results have been revealed in Wales. Verheyen, in Belgium, also joins in this chorus.[11] A French author writes: "Polyglottism is incontestably an obstacle to ideation. This fact, of capital importance, is misunderstood by many psychologists and pedagogues."[12]

In spite of the discouraging character of these studies, bilingualism or multilingualism must be the lot of many countries and provinces for a long time to come. A vital immediate problem in these regions is how best to handle the situation. On this point the conclusions are nearly unanimous; namely, that the active use of the second language in instruction be deferred at least until the age of nine.

In 1902 a commission was appointed to study the school situation in the Acadian district of Canada. The following paragraph summarizes the conclusion:

Your commissioners find that the fundamental error in dealing with the French schools, which must be held responsible for many of their shortcomings, has been the assumption that they must be taught exclusively in English. They find that, with startling uniformity and persistency, attempts have been made to educate children from French speaking homes and with none but French speaking playmates by means of the English language alone, sometimes from the lips of teachers who can speak nothing but English. They find from the testimony of experts that, even were such teachers masters of the most approved modern methods of teaching a foreign language, but meager results could be anticipated from their best efforts under such conditions. They find that with the inexperienced, ill-taught, and often otherwise incompetent teachers ordinarily available for employment in such schools, the efforts, however conscientious, made to teach the children to speak English are, as might be anticipated, largely a failure. They find also that, while futile attempts to teach them English are thus being put forth, the general education of French speaking pupils is being more or less seriously or sometimes even totally neglected.[18]

In all discussions of bilingualism it must be understood that only the active use of the language, that is, speaking knowledge, is involved. Few have claimed that there are any seriously harmful effects from learning to read a dozen or more languages. The psychological processes involved are essentially different.

Speaking knowledge demands the creation of reflexes: it is the difference between recognizing how an automobile is driven and the establishment of the necessary habits involved in actual driving. It is the difference between recognizing a swan-dive and being able to do it, or seeing how a typewriter is operated by the touch system and the training of the fingers to act automatically. An active use of a language demands the creation of habits by almost infinite repetition, the changing of a whole symbolic system within the mind or the addition of another complete system, so that the thought itself is carried on in the foreign medium. To accomplish this task, which increases with the richness of the content of the mind, requires practice and time which might be used to develop a single symbolic or conceptual system. One cannot repeat too often that facility in learning to speak depends upon how much there is to express, and that thought and language develop together and, practically speaking, are inseparable.

As a general proposition we can state (with Michael West) that the reduction of the *expressive* study of foreign languages (except where special needs exist) is relief from an economic, hygienic, and intellectual burden. To read several languages, but to speak only one, to be an active monoglot, a passive polyglot—this is about the only generalized precept the present knowledge of the subject permits.[14]

BILINGUALISM FROM AN AMERICAN VIEWPOINT

Bilingualism as a national problem, however interesting in itself, concerns us in America very little. Still, in view of the efforts in many schools to teach a foreign language as an expressive function, the possible effect of complete or considerable success (something not to be feared at present) is worth noting.

If a student's normal vocabulary is 25,000 items, learning a new foreign language effectively means an additional series of 25,000 duplicates, not counting the grammatical patterns involved. The difficulty of speaking four or five languages can easily be estimated. Attention may be diverted from new things and experiences in the real world toward new foreign designations for old objects and experiences. Minds may become so stuffed with words that thought becomes difficult. There are individuals who have learned actively so many languages that they can say nothing of importance in any, including their native tongue.

For every gain made in one language used actively, there is usually a loss in the other. In general, as Smith points out, the loss is double: "on the one hand the development of ideas is hindered and on the other the power of expression is limited." [15]

For those who study languages to be able to read them only, no serious complaints can be made. The process involved, as has been pointed out, is fundamentally different. If French, for instance, is read constantly, the principal interference is in spelling and punctuation. The reader of this language may have to look up "responsibility" about every time he writes it because of *responsable;* he has to be careful, moreover, about "address" and *adresse,* "dance" and *danse,* "resemble" and *ressembler,* "apartment" and *appartement,* "ecstasy" and *extase,* and so on with forty or fifty common items.

This interference is not serious in itself, but serves to illustrate the maze of conflicts involved in speaking or in writing (not just *reading*) a foreign tongue. Everyone knows the influence of native pronunciation on foreign sounds, and this is typical of the confusions everywhere, in singulars and plurals (Eng., "to make progress," Fr., "to make progresses," *faire des progrès;* Eng., "information," Fr., "informations," *des renseignements,* and so on); in syntax (Eng., "since I have been here," Fr., "since I am here," *depuis que je suis ici);* in figurative distinctions ("a pig," *un cochon*); and so on. The ramifications and complications, irrationalities and confusions are infinite ("a cynic," *un cynique),* so that anyone can see what a tight rope a foreign language speaker must walk. Often he succeeds by not venturing far from the simplest, commonplace formulas.

If it is true, as many have maintained, that active bi- or multi-lingualism is a burden to the mind rather than a help, only urgent practical needs could justify *required* courses directed seriously toward this end. Fortunately, in the United States, the degree of bilingualism acquired in school by any method is so slight that no occasion for alarm exists. Sometimes the only issue involved is learning *something* (and thus keeping the mind active) versus learning nothing at all. The serious complaint is rather against the waste and relative futility of many of such efforts.

III

The Present Disorder

1. READING VERSUS SPEAKING

ENOUGH HAS BEEN said already to illustrate the great difference in character and difficulty between reading knowledge of a foreign language and speaking knowledge. Considered as a school discipline, that is, as an educative influence, reading knowledge, in contrast to speaking knowledge, requires a more exclusive exercise of the intellectual faculties. The one demands constant learning, the other constant repetition or "over-learning." The one does not place the thoughtful, original, and introverted under such serious handicaps. Reading knowledge belongs with such subjects as arithmetic and geometry, which for centuries have been considered as means for developing minds, in contrast with more practical courses which involve skills primarily.

Nothing in this indicates that speaking knowledge as an aim is not legitimate in many situations. The matter is viewed here from the viewpoint of curriculum-making in public schools and colleges—that is, from considerations of what might be so generally useful as to be required of all students. Courses in conversational or commercial French (Spanish, Italian, German, etc.) should be offered for future teachers and for others who have an immediate practical need: they should not form a part of the requirements for all students or be substituted for the requirements.

Many language teachers will have difficulty in accepting this view. They are a selected group, and the selection has eliminated some who might incline toward this opinion. Those who disagree can present a number of arguments.

SOME ARGUMENTS FOR SPEAKING KNOWLEDGE

The least serious argument for emphasizing the spoken language is that "the best and quickest means to learn to read is to learn to speak."

In every great error there is usually an element of truth, but the truth here is exceptionally slight. To understand all the fine points about acrobatics, professional baseball or football, or any other complicated and difficult skill, there is no training, certainly, equivalent to participating actively in these exercises. But life is short, and the millions who attend baseball and football contests have other concerns, and almost no one, before attending a game or before watching the feats of aviators and high divers, feels obliged to try out these activities. To be an expert and to pronounce judgments, the authority of this training is necessary; and this is doubtless the element of truth in the error.

To assume that speaking knowledge is the only way to learn to read would be altogether too fantastic. Hardly a student has gone through French, Latin, or German courses in school without realizing the relatively broad extent of his passive knowledge, the pitifully small extent of his expressive ability. The relative difficulty of the two attainments is, perhaps, as fifteen or twenty to one. If reading knowledge is the aim, the waste involved in purely oral methods is considerable. Theoretically that might mean reduplicating the student's linguistic and mental growth.

A more serious argument, often made, for stressing the spoken language is that pupils and parents want it. Speaking a foreign tongue is interesting; it enlivens the class work; it seems real, tangible, something definitely gained, something that can be shown. All this is true. There is not an intellectual activity in school or outside that most people will not evade if they possibly can. If geometry could be presented in connection with dance forms and there were a choice between abstract geometry and applied, nearly all students would choose the applied form. They would have little knowledge of geometry and considerable knowledge of an esoteric dance—but what would they do with their curious dancing afterwards? There is a slight analogy with language instruction.

While the interest that an active use of the foreign language causes is real, especially at first, it is an interest that, for unselected groups, soon fades. Nothing delights a class more for a few days than to find a professor who doesn't speak a word of English, who gesticulates and displays histrionic talent. The student can remain passive in the hope of absorbing knowledge.

It is true that there is such a thing as passive learning: by long familiarity with and almost unconscious absorption of little details one gets an historical sense, or learns to distinguish the classic from the romantic. But this educational method is abused when concrete facts are involved —the forms of a verb, the multiplication table, or the series of atomic weights. Nothing is more wasteful or discouraging than to try to memorize this kind of material when half awake.

Thus, if the show continues entirely painless, it becomes

monotonous and almost useless. If progress is insisted upon, then work, hard, unpleasant work, is the accompaniment.

NEED FOR CANDOR

The majority of teachers stress mainly the written language, consciously or subconsciously, but keep the aim of speaking knowledge as a kind of pretense. They would be almost afraid to do otherwise. They know that if courses were divided (as they might well be) into literary French, and practical, spoken French, most of the students would flock to the latter variety, other things being equal. But this lack of decision and candor has created an unhealthy situation, so that a concerted attack has been made against all language study, which is being threatened more and more with banishment from the required curriculum.

The situation must be faced. The attempt to compromise between the merely practical and the broadly educational viewpoints leads only to confusion. Courses in commercial Spanish or in conversational French should be offered for those who need them, or even for those who merely think they have this need, but these courses should not be required.

In many cases the practical advantage of foreign language study can hardly be presented without deception. The skill imparted in most schools will always be, as now, too imperfect. Moreover, as a money-making accomplishment, an active knowledge of a foreign language (which takes years to acquire in school under the most favorable circumstances) can never compete with bookkeeping, accounting, business practice, personnel direction, chemistry, advertising, and other skills. The students turned out from courses in commercial Spanish each year, even if competent, would supply the need for native Americans in that work (that is, as correspondents) for a generation. And of a hundred thousand who have learned French conversational phrases (e.g. *Madame est-elle visible?* or *Où est la douane?*) only a minute percentage ever finds under normal conditions any urgent or inescapable need for this knowledge, or ever profits or saves a dollar through it.

IMMATURITY OF STUDENTS

A still further and generalized argument in favor of the spoken language, especially in the beginning, is that pupils are too immature for a more formalized and organized study of foreign languages. That is perhaps true in some high schools, and a totally new type of language course might be more profitable. In other cases this objection is rather a criticism of the grammars and other books in general use. The subject matter is always difficult in the sense that it is vast; but the textbooks can proceed rapidly or slowly, be easy or difficult, regardless of the aim. If reading knowledge becomes the exclusive aim of the instruction in elementary classes, the type of textbooks in current use must be greatly modified.

In the proposals of this book nothing drastic is necessarily intended. There are always many students in high school and in college for whom formal study in the traditional sense is unprofitable. They cannot really understand anything, whether art, literature, or thought; but they can acquire skills. They might just as well waste time on commercial Spanish as on Racine, whom they could never understand anyway. Until the realization spreads that formal education cannot correct the errors of nature and heredity, that a college degree may lead to nothing and, on the other hand, that most useful skills can best be acquired in industry and in business—until this understanding becomes widespread, it is necessary to compromise and to wait. But there should be an end of self-deceptions and deceptions of others.

One more point must be mentioned. While reading knowledge that implies the ability to understand Molière, say, or Pascal, is not the most efficient means to learn how to order a dinner in Paris, still it is not unrelated to practical, speaking knowledge. It can form the basis and the background for that knowledge. A person who can read a foreign tongue has a tremendous head start over one who knows nothing at all. The transition to speaking ability comes fast when the need arises and practice begins. Usually a student with such knowledge will go farther in the end in the practical use of language than one who has confined himself to a series of conversational phrases.

The advantage of reading knowledge in this respect is obvious: what is generally useful comes first, what is possible and contingent is left for the possibility or contingency to arise.

2. OBJECTIONS TO ALL LANGUAGE STUDY

Besides the objections to speaking knowledge as an aim in required courses, there are some complaints against all language study to which I do not wholly subscribe, but which are worth mentioning as dangers to be avoided or to be compensated for.

A first complaint, often made, is that in unfavorable circumstances language study, like many other formal disciplines, may divert attention from things to words and thus contribute to the verbalism from which the world has long been suffering. A French writer asserts that the mind is enriched more by experience with things than by the memorizing of verbal equivalents for those things in several languages. It is more useful, he says, to know how to distinguish between the leaves of different trees than to know the equivalent of the word "tree" in five languages. He goes further and states that the least experiment in physics or chemistry furnishes more material for the intelligence to work on than a literary passage in a foreign tongue dealing with things already known to the child. "One can hardly realize what verbalism in general and the prejudice in favor of language study in particular have cost and still cost humanity." [1]

The indictment is drawn up by Mr. Charles Mercier as follows:

The devotion of disproportionate time and attention to languages, whether living or dead, is not merely waste, it is actively pernicious and baneful. It does irreparable harm to the growing mind. It fosters and increases that logolatry, that inability to distinguish between words and things, that pseudo-solution of problems by the invention of neat phrases that goes by the name of learning.[2]

Some have claimed that the memory work necessary in language study has been positively disadvantageous to them. One such critic writes, "Learning by heart the Greek grammar did me harm, a great deal of harm. While I was doing it, the observing and reflective powers lay dormant, indeed, they were systematically suppressed." [3]

These quotations are cited not as a final word on the subject, but merely as indicating complaints that have been made.

DISLIKE OF LANGUAGE STUDY

One investigator has found that almost ninety per cent of those who have studied a modern foreign language for two or more years indicate a distaste for the subject.[4] If students were left entirely free in the choice of their studies, it is likely that only a small proportion would choose any foreign language. This in itself does not mean very much, since students would hardly go to school at all if no suggestive or compulsive forces were at work. Nevertheless the relatively great dislike for language study does create a special situation. The forced feeding produces resistances, indigestions, and various other mental disturbances. The subject is disliked before its advantages can be appreciated; and student resistances can defeat many aims. Students practice evasions, sometimes countenanced. Many of them become so inured to error and nonsense that they fall into delirious interpretations without batting an eye.[5]

Language study is inevitably rigorous, but some of its value may also lie in that fact. Any study which involves a new symbolism is difficult and is acquired with a certain amount of painful effort, whether the symbolism is linguistic, mathematical, or what not. The trouble is due, not so much to inherent difficulties in the notations, as to the cumulative nature of such study. In history or social science a student can miss a lesson here and there without grave damage. In language study, if he misses one, those following become doubly difficult, and if he misses many, he is soon completely lost.

Although part of the hostility toward language study is due to a desire to avoid any discipline that is rigorous, steady, and cumulative, a still greater part is a result of the confusions in aims and the inefficiency of the instruction, matters that will be dealt with later. The dislike of language study as administered at present is no argument against its real value under favorable conditions. It is merely a symptom that something may be wrong somewhere.

3. DISORGANIZATION OF LANGUAGE DEPARTMENTS

In the Middle Ages whole realms of human knowledge were embraced under an all-inclusive heading. As late as the eighteenth century, "natural philosophy" included chemistry, physics, botany, and the rest of the natural sciences. These enormous territories have been divided and to some extent conquered, but "French," for example, remains as it has been—a vast field demanding the most varied as well as contradictory talents.

The professor of a foreign language in college is engaged in a variety of pursuits. He may be, for instance,

1. A scientist, dealing principally with experimental phonetics.
2. A practitioner of the art of noting and reproducing sounds.
3. A literary or cultural historian, a biographer, a historian of forms and manners, a critic (objective, subjective, or impressionistic), an editor of texts.
4. A philologist, lexicographer, phonologist, antiquarian, paleographer.
5. An interpreter of literature, an actor, performer, elocutionist, esthetician, prosodist, collector and interpreter of folk ways.
6. A teacher of oral French, written French, literary French, conversational French, scientific French, commercial French, *ad lib.*, and of all the subject matters mentioned above.

To speak of the qualities necessary for this profession is to speak of a kind of infinity.[6]

The classification above is by no means exhaustive. Literature alone embraces a universe. It may be poetical; and poetry may be philosophical, narrative, lyric, didactic, popular, humorous, hypnotic, or nonsensical. Varieties of literature range from Mother Goose to the Divine Comedy. The novel and the drama are special fields. There is also the literature of criticism, religious literature, philosophical writing, travel, biography, memoirs, and scientific literature.

To gain a license to teach any of these varied branches of either language or literature the candidate must usually have some rather deep knowledge about one. In some cases, the situation would hardly be different if Ph.D's in chemistry were commissioned to teach archaeology. To grant a permit to teach French literature on the basis of a study of the glottis or of the syntax of Rhaeto-Romance is like giving a license to practice medicine for a thesis on the origin and properties of the madstone.

This criticism has been made frequently. As Arthur Livingston has said:

> The modern language teacher in the American university finds himself struggling to do three things, each one of which constitutes a special profession by itself. He tries to be a scientist in the field of philology and ultimately in the field of history. He is forced by necessity, by interest and tradition to become a critic and a student of literature. He makes his bread by pedagogy, in imparting the spoken language.[7]

CONFUSION IN AIMS

A far more serious matter is the diversity of aims and of emphasis in the elementary courses. One manual for teachers defines the purposes of modern language teaching in terms of the following: (1) purposive and abstract thinking (*sic*); (2) the power to read; (3) an understanding of the life, art, institutions, religion, and politics of the foreign country; (4) the ability to speak and understand the foreign tongue; (5) the ability to write the foreign tongue; (6) comprehension of and power to use English grammar, including syntax; (7) a tool for the prosecution of other studies; (8) interpretation of foreign abbreviations, phrases and quotations; and (9) "general habits and ideals of greatest value."

In another paragraph this author mentions "good will to men," "ideals of social behavior, honor, justice, courage, etc.," and "moral aspects." Obviously, nearly everything in the universe of intellectual and moral values is included.[8]

What is important is not the number of aims, but their sequence. When the student and teacher are distracted between love of humanity as a goal and the forms of the participles, both ends are apt to suffer. Perhaps some of the dislike of foreign language study is due to the constant disorientation of the student and the vagueness of the objective.

Leaving aside all incidental gains and considering only reading and speaking, there are still numerous ambiguities that prevent knowing just what to do. The very term "reading knowledge" and "speaking knowledge" have no precise meaning. To an American who once asked the inevitable question, "Do you speak English?" Coppée is reported to have replied: "No, madam, I am still learning French."[9] Likewise Goethe stated that he had been learning to read for eighty years and was still not satisfied with his progress.

What is French?—It is a language, of course, but whose language? Is it the language of an average child, an educated adult, or of a literary artist? Is it the written language or the spoken language?—the language of the classical dramatists or of the romantic word-painters? If it is the language of science, which science?—and so on.

Any language is infinite: no one can know it all, and a choice must be made.

Within each tongue there are numerous spoken languages and numerous written languages. It is quite possible to know the written language and not the spoken, and vice versa. We are all lost in some fields of discourse. A treatise on mathematics is usually beyond the comprehension of any one except a mathematician. In certain matters, such as dressmaking and cosmetics, half the population is more or less at sea on the basis of sex differentiation alone.

The magnitude of the task of learning how to read or to speak absolutely can be understood by looking at a dictionary. The new Webster contains, alas! 600,000 words, and these include only a fraction of scientific terminology. To know a language in an absolute sense would be to know the sum of a race's thought and experience. Some single items, such as "romanticism" or "economic determinism" can hardly be explained in less than a long article or book.

In addition to the ambiguities concerning "reading knowledge" and "speaking knowledge," there is also the matter of literature, infinite in its variety and scope—simple and obscure, mature and immature, classic and romantic. All this, and much more, is serenely grouped under "French" or "German." It is doubtful if most teachers have a clear idea of just what they are to teach.

Many classroom practices illustrate the confusion. A typical elementary class engages in the following: practice in hearing French, practice in speaking French, practice in writing French, practice in translating from French to English and vice versa, all this with relatively little attention (although word counts have offered some help) to what French is to be heard, written, spoken, and translated.

This routine is varied by reading from literary authors who take liberties with the tongue, who perform as virtuosos for an audience that already knows the language, certainly not for foreign students trying to learn it. Far from having a direct relation to the study of the language, this literary study may help to defeat the language aim. The memory is burdened with unimportant synonyms and with emotive and figurative uses of words that obscure primary meanings.

Mr. E. A. Kirkpatrick has described the situation as follows:

It would be just as sensible to offer a course on automobiles which should include the structure and repair of autos, how to drive them, their social significance and the most artistic way of designing and painting them as it is to offer a course in French which covers French grammar, the reading and speaking of French, a social study of the French people, and training and appreciation of French literature.[10]

NEED FOR SPECIFIC COURSES

If courses in language were rationally organized, there would be courses in oral French, similar perhaps to those of the Berlitz schools, for those who have or think they have special needs. There would be courses in reading French in which all attention would be paid to learning vocabulary items in order of their importance (frequency of occurrence)—a study uncomplicated by literary concerns. There would be courses in literature including both the reading of texts, and the study of literary and cultural history.

For students in high school, a required course might be

devoted to common root words in Greek, Latin, French, German, and Italian, with a study of prefixes and suffixes, and the English derivatives of these words.[11]

A first advantage of this limitation in scope would be to give the teacher a more precise idea of what to do, and the problem of methodology would be greatly simplified. That problem would not be, as now, how to teach in a unified effort matters as disparate as ideals and interjections. The students might gain new interest. They could see where they were going. At present a student may imagine he is to learn how to talk the foreign language and then discover that most of his work has little to do with speaking. His parents are likewise deceived and wonder why, after years of study, he can neither speak, read, nor write.

To create the reflexes involved in the active use of such phrases as *ne le lui a-t-il pas donné* requires perhaps twenty times as much effort and practice as learning to interpret them when written. To learn the gender of each of thousands of nouns in French requires an immense amount of effort; to read, it is hardly necessary to know the gender of a single one. Yet a student who may have no other purpose than to learn to interpret the written language must, because of this confusion in aims, spend hours learning genders and the placing of conjunctive pronouns in order. The loss is greater even than the time wasted, since the student is disoriented and discouraged. Consider what this loss means in the life of a student taking required courses in foreign languages year after year. Then multiply this one individual's loss by two or three or four hundred thousand, and you will have some idea of what is involved.

HOW TO DEFINE "READING KNOWLEDGE"

The appearance a few years ago of lists of word frequencies, in spite of certain errors and limitations in those lists, has made possible an expedient definition of reading knowledge. This acquirement might be considered as the ability to recognize in context the first two or three thousand words of a frequency list. This would imply, in the case of most languages studied, a total vocabulary of many thousands of words, since learned and technical terms, which are of lower frequency, are recognizable at first sight by anyone who knows them in the vernacular. Or, "reading knowledge" could be recognized frankly as a variable, but fixed in any given case by a number which would indicate a point on the scale, e.g., student Jones, French reading knowledge, 5; Smith, 10, the numbers standing for the point in thousands on the frequency list.

This method, or this understanding, would give some meaning to the term which it lacks entirely at present. Graduate schools and various departments specify frequently, in a kind of despair, "a reading knowledge of French or German," hoping, apparently, that someone (not themselves) will understand approximately what they mean. Whether a student is found to have this vague ability or not depends at present partly on the temperament or digestion of the examiner.

This would be a first step in giving precision to the aims, and the first aim should be reading knowledge as conventionally determined, that is, in terms of the first two or three thousand words of the frequency list, plus a certain number of items from the idiom list. Thus the task to be accomplished would be defined almost as rigorously as the multiplication table, and methodologists might experiment to determine with finality what methods of presentation are relatively most economical of effort. This economy of effort admits of scientific, experimental measurement. Thus a science of language pedagogy could replace the numerous present competing philosophies.

The second aim of the required courses should be to present the character and values, that is, the "culture" of the foreign civilization as represented in its literature. For practical purposes, and to avoid a merely rhetorical exercise, that culture might be defined expediently in terms of a list of representative works, just as the linguistic aim is defined in terms of concrete items.

With this understanding of the aims and nature of the required courses, it is possible to present an apology for them without denying the criticisms that have been made and without approving all that is being done at present.

Part Two
A DEFENSE OF FOREIGN LANGUAGE STUDY

IV

Why Study a Foreign Language?

THE FIRST REASON for making foreign language study a required discipline is that language itself is important, and the only way to understand language, our own or any other, is through a foreign medium.

The importance of our tongue is always casually admitted, but seldom deeply felt. Language is as vital as any or even all other subjects. We live in two universes, a universe of *things,* with which science deals, and in a universe of *communication.* We are constantly talking or constantly listening. When no one is around to hear our remarks, we talk to ourselves—we think or dream.

Words are the means by which our civilization is developed, maintained, and passed on. Our language determines largely the character of our intelligence, our loyalties and disloyalties. We live in words, we are surrounded by them, they line the streets, they now fill the air. And the only means we have to get outside of our own language so that we can even look at it is through foreign language study.

No one can know the characteristics of his own language, its features, its defects, its qualities without understanding another tongue. Qualities exist only in relationships; nothing is high or low, good or bad, except by comparison with something else. A foreign language furnishes a term of comparison.

Languages have distinct and diverse characters: they are as different as faces. German looks different, sounds different, feels different from French. The very exercises in French, in German, in Italian, and in Spanish vary in character. Some seem straightforward, direct, clear; others have a sympathetic homeliness; still others have sounds that reflect clear skies. Latin can suggest even to a small boy the order and weight of the legions. Only by being aware of the quality of another tongue can we have even an idea about the character of our own.

Through foreign language study a person perceives how conventional language is, and he becomes conscious for the first time of the mechanism of his own speech. The Englishman who considered the French a silly people because they call their mothers "mares" and their daughters "fillies" represents an extreme, but natural, linguistic ignorance. Without knowledge of a foreign language we are caught in our verbal subjectivism, like a squirrel in his cage. Labels, sounds appear to have a direct, immediate, and logical relationship to what they symbolize; things and symbols are confused in what may be, and often is, the worst of confusions.

Some curriculum-makers regard elementary language work merely as a preparation, as furnishing a tool for which there is no use unless the student goes farther and absorbs the thought or literature of the foreign country. The contrary viewpoint would be equally plausible, namely, that the ideas, customs, history, and literature of the foreign country can be presented in English, whereas the language, the characteristics of mind that language objectifies, can be known only by a study of the medium itself.

WHY STUDY A FOREIGN LANGUAGE?

Elementary language work plunges the student suddenly into a new mental atmosphere. Almost from the first day he senses the quality of the language he is studying. The vocabulary, the sound and order of the words, their method of composition and derivation—all that is a new world in which other minds—millions of them—live and have lived.

MENTAL DISCIPLINE

A tendency nowadays is to discount all claims for mental discipline except in relation to exactly similar skills or activities. Yet, to give up these claims entirely would be to reject most of the traditional subjects of the curriculum. Who uses algebra, trigonometry, ancient history, Latin, chemistry, etc., directly or indirectly in his daily life? Almost no one. And yet these disciplines (plus many other factors) apparently effect changes so noticeable that a few minutes of casual conversation usually suffice to identify a man who has had this kind of training. The difference is as real as that between the average lawyer and the average plumber. Whether the cause is labeled "mental discipline," "education," or something else, is unimportant. Studies that permit little direct transfer of training do change and distinguish.

Language study exercises the memory almost exclusively; but memory cannot be divorced entirely from other intellectual faculties. It depends on and is facilitated by close observation of resemblances, differences, distinctions. The ability to perceive such differences and resemblances characterizes most mental development.

In language study no bluff, no rationalizing will do. You are almost always either right or wrong without appeal. The study enforces meticulous observation, careful attention to details. Perhaps no transfer of carefulness is possible

—we will not argue this point. But a student can discover, if only as a matter of knowledge, that in the use of words, little things (e.g. tense distinctions) really count.

It is quite likely that any honest, careful, intellectual activity is educative in almost any sense in which that term may be taken, and that being educated, as we say, is the result of a coöperative effort in which many teachers and many different subject matters take part. This thought should incline the opponents of language study to a certain tolerance. To confine students to foreign languages could hardly be recommended by any one, although as an exclusive discipline language study has had further trial than almost any other, and has accompanied certainly the longest list of distinguished minds.

THE MOTHER TONGUE

For improving a student's use and detailed knowledge of the mother tongue, courses aimed directly at that goal would probably be more effective than a dependence upon the incidental gains of ordinary foreign language study. But in the lack of such courses much knowledge of English must be gained through a study of Latin or of one of the Romanic tongues. It is hardly necessary to mention that if a student knows *aqua*, "aquarium," "aquatic," "aqueduct," "aquatint," "aqueous," and even "aquacade" become understandable.

In this connection, it is a curious fact that most of the great writers the world has known, from Cicero on down, have attended schools in which foreign language training was one of the principal (if not the principal) disciplines. Here there may be no relationship of cause and effect, but the fact is at least a curious coincidence. Whatever the cause, common observation shows that graduates of the classical curriculum of Oxford or Cambridge and of Arts colleges in America usually do better in English than veterinarians, agronomists, and others whose foreign language study has generally been neglected—a fact that selection and environment alone do not wholly explain.

COMPARISON WITH OTHER SUBJECTS

In addition to the gains that relate to the foreign language itself, some connected discourse, some books will be read in the very process of teaching how to read. This involves other matters, namely, the value of foreign language courses in comparison with those in English literature, comparative literature, history, and, perhaps, even the social sciences.

Courses in comparative literature can take the place of much foreign language study, but cannot replace that study wholly. Anything that is read for content primarily can be translated, and that is more than is generally supposed. Many philosophical, narrative, and dramatic poets can be handled in English translation: the works that defy foreign renderings are mainly those that are lyric, suggestive, or evocative. It is practically impossible to put Shakespeare into a Romance tongue, to give the equivalent of the English psalms, or to translate the lyric poets of any country, except, perhaps, in the case of languages closely related. The simplest things, curiously, are the most difficult to translate—the flavor of words, the associations of words and emotions. In nearly every translation of a literary work something is lost, but, in certain cases, the loss may be very little and more than compensated for by the saving in time and effort.

It is never possible, however, to enter fully into the spirit of another nation except through its language. To depend on translations is like studying the colorless reproductions of paintings rather than the originals in galleries. When the galleries are too difficult of access, the reproductions may be most useful, but they never satisfy wholly. While many works can be handled in translation almost as well as in the original, if attention centers on what is universal in them, not special and particular, it is still impossible to know a foreign race intimately except through its language. It is the difference between knowing a man through a photograph and knowing him by living with him.

While comparative literature deserves a larger place in the curriculum than it has, its function is to supplement and complete rather than to take the place of foreign language study. In the decline of Latin and Greek, it would be disastrous if all that those civilizations stood for should be ignored and forgotten.

ENGLISH COURSES

Courses in English and in English literature do not take the place of world literature or the study of literature in a foreign language. There is no way even to judge English literature without a means of comparison. Those who confine themselves to that study, specializing more and more in third- and fourth- and fifth-rate writers are, without a term of comparison, incapable of a qualitative judgment concerning any literature including their own. Farquhar has one stature standing beside Wycherley, and another when standing beside Molière, Goldoni, or Aristophanes. It is like studying music and leaving out Bach, Beethoven, Hayden, Scarlatti, Brahms, Debussy, and Wagner; or painting without the Italian or Flemish schools.

An exclusive devotion to English is particularly unfortunate since all of us are surrounded by English standards, English viewpoints, English ideas, and English art. The influence comes with the type of cooking, with Puritanism, Victorianism, and Horatio Alger. We absorb English influences through all our pores. Over-emphasis on English causes a grotesque distortion: the place of English literature in world literature, the position of England (an honorable one) in the history of civilization—all that is apt to be magnified in our minds. Why cultivate this Narcissism, why gaze so exclusively at our own image, at the expression of ourselves? If this is broadening and educative, to the point where it is carried, then it is hard to know what broadening is.

Opponents of foreign language study seldom attack courses in English: not a murmur, not a word is heard. The reason is apparent. Whenever a student's paper comes in misspelled, badly organized, incoherent, irrational, the busy scientist or technician concludes, not that past English study was ineffective, but that more is needed. He fails to realize that in the business of teaching how to think, which is usually involved in these gross disorders, every one cooperates, and in many cases it would be as reasonable to prescribe a rigorous course in economic thinking as to demand another course in Donne, Wycherley, or *The Faerie Queene*. But this is how it is.

IMPORTANCE OF LITERATURE

The question may arise as to whether any literary courses should be required, whether required instruction should not be confined to science, mathematics, history, and philosophy—just what would the loss be? In many cases candor compels the answer: There would be none. With some students, ideas and cultural influences are like water on a duck's back. But in the scheme of education as it has been generally understood or sensed, such study is at the very core. To abolish it would be to change everything.

The attack on foreign language study comes largely from proponents of the social sciences who, in this revolutionary period, are feeling their oats and want more room. This is natural and honest enough, and the complaint against *some* language study is more than justified. But frequently the attack comes from those who have no understanding of what literature is or of its importance.

Literature is more than versification, amusement, eloquence, and fiction. It involves almost the sum of what a nation has thought about religion, economics, society, the arts, the good life for man, the pleasures and elegances of life. It is one of the major forces in the lives of all of us. What school and college courses can do in determining how people act and live is negligible in comparison with the effect even of popular literature. Where do girls learn with what conventions or with what armor to greet their suitors? Where do they get their ideas of what the good life is, what counts for happiness, the current and fashionable coquetries in language and manners? They acquire all this from the novels they read, the plays they see, the movies they attend. We delude ourselves, all of us, if we think our courses can compete on a large scale with these suggestive influences. The best we can do is to work with small groups that later may help to provide the literature and to establish the prestige values, and to combat in this way the commercial panders.

This must be clear: that literature, whether popular or any other kind, is not unimportant, not a special province, not something that concerns only an esoteric few.

A parent not content that his son or daughter should live

in the sterile atmosphere of Hollywood might decide to send him or her traveling through the world. The experience would be broadly educative in a universally accepted sense. The child could see what other races consider important and unimportant, could compare the elegance of Hollywood with polite society elsewhere. But that traveling is not possible for everyone, and, fortunately, is not necessary.

UNDERSTANDING SOCIAL PATTERNS

Of the two kinds of traveling, that done in books can be far superior. It is possible to go around the world and not see more than could be observed in the lobby of a New York hotel. Whatever a nation really stands for, whatever is important in its life and civilization, reaches consciousness only in the heads of a small minority, the artists and intellectuals. A traveler in France may observe little except bad plumbing and rapacious trading; to find what French civilization stands for, he must look for those who represent it.

The traveling that study of foreign literature permits is not only a horizontal displacement in space, but also a vertical displacement in time. It allows us to escape from the atmosphere of the home, the village, the parish, and from the styles, fads, and fancies, not only of a single place, but of a single epoch.

Without knowledge of other ages and other civilizations we can be eminent specialists in science and still know almost nothing about the world we are living in. We have no way to compare our folk-ways and beliefs with others, and thus what is merely conventional and passing, we are apt to take as constant, natural, and eternal. Religions, moralities, and political faiths change almost from year to year, and yet they seem to us absolute and final. Popular ideas of pretty clothes and faces, which we attribute to an innate aesthetic sense, are apt to come from the magazine covers and are so inconstant that we laugh at pictures on issues barely ten years old. The touching scenes of the silent movies now make the same audiences roar. The central problem of the intellectual life is to get out of the atmosphere of conventions in which we live. How else can we judge them, look at them, understand them, and not be victims of the constant suggestive influences around us?

It is easy to go beyond realities in this matter and envision in lyric terms what it means to live in all ages and in all societies. The majority of students are born with short breath and small wings. But this curse limits what they can gain from any study. And, in most cases, there is some reaction—a student can finish Sophocles and still prefer Tarzan, but he is a bit troubled by the difference, not so comfortable in his admiration as before.

HISTORY

History can contribute as much, perhaps, as the study of foreign literature to this enlargement of one's world. But the historian places emphasis on developments in government and institutions, and on the framework within which life is carried on. The literature of a period represents the intimate life of the age. It expresses the aspirations of the best minds, the moralities and immoralities, what is valued and not valued. For a complete historical sense, one study must supplement the other. Consider what the Greek drama reveals concerning the manners, customs, politeness, superstitions, and cruelties of the age and place in which it was written, and what the literature of the French seventeenth century may contribute toward an understanding of politeness, taste, and manners. The past may be the only means by which we can understand the present, judge it, and plan the future.

NATURAL SCIENCE

The position of the natural scientists in this warfare over the curriculum is quite secure. Science is too useful, its merited prestige is too great. Rather than sacrifice the scientific method, all the poetry in the world could better be dispensed with. The peculiar advantage of science, however, is that its method is relatively fool-proof, and it can show fewer failures, therefore, than other disciplines. Those who have been called "the little men of science," without ideas, without originality, incapable of important discoveries or syntheses, can always be useful as experts and technicians in small matters, without having an intellectual range that covers much more than the sports page.

But the record of the natural sciences as a general or exclusive educational discipline is neither long nor conclusive. Most thoughtful scientists recognize that their field is limited, that a world of communication, of customs, of moralities, and of values exists quite outside the scope of their own method, and that this universe is as important as the physical world in which we live.

THE SOCIAL SCIENCES

In spite of superficial advantages, the position of the social scientists is far less secure. A plain man confronted with a curriculum consisting of government, economics, marriage, citizenship, etc., on the one hand, and Greek drama, Latin conjugations, trigonometry, and the history of Egypt on the other, would hardly hesitate in his choice.

The first subjects are, after all, the important things. Without other considerations we must all agree: government is more important than Virgil's eclogues; marriage is more vital than the Hôtel de Rambouillet; economics more significant than preciosity or *marivaudage.*

The question, however, is not altogether *if* these subjects are important, but also *when* they are important. If you regard life as ending with the curriculum, there must be eagerness to present what has been discovered in the social sciences and the methods used in the discovery. But life is long. Social science is not one of the subjects that must be studied first.

If students do not acquire in school a background, a symbolism, and a training in rigorous scientific or verbal thinking, they can never make up the loss. But social science, on the other hand, can and should occupy trained minds for the rest of their lives. The questions involved are interesting, popular, and important. They are within the province of adult education, and publicists, writers, and statesmen all deal with them. Books for nearly every class of readers are available in most libraries. A student who does not study Virgil in school is not likely ever to know much about him; but this is not true of those who offer, not a discipline, but a revelation.

As an occasion for mental training, the social sciences seldom compare in rigor with other subjects. Many of them are notoriously easy. They involve no elaborate symbolism. In contrast to foreign language study, rigorous tests for understanding are more difficult to devise and to apply. A student in social science can learn a verbal formula or explanation by rote without knowing more about the matter than he does about a medieval salamander. On examination he sends these formulas back to the professor who

WHY STUDY A FOREIGN LANGUAGE?

reads and comments "How true!" This is not always the case, of course, but it is always a possibility.

It is hardly time for the social sciences to supplant linguistic and literary study as the foundation courses in college. Their methods are barely established, their record, bad. They are almost never free: they must accept broadly and generally the catechisms, values, and moralities approved by the groups who control and probably always will control all societies. Thus the gospel of Adam Smith had respectability—it was approved by bankers and industrialists; the gospel of Veblen drove its prophet from pillar to post.

Some have maintained that the most developed of the social sciences, namely economics, has done more harm in the world than good. During the nineteenth century and in a part of this century it existed mainly as a rationalization and apology for an economic system that was beginning to revolt all enlightened consciences.

It is possible to go further and to state that without a deep historical sense, a feeling for the values and aspirations of other ages, social science is bound to do more harm than good. If *Middletown* can be believed, this subject as taught in high school is a silly catechism presented by bewildered girls to equally bewildered pupils.

Social sciences are almost necessarily based on assumptions of value. These are usually the values of a particular time and place accepted as constant and eternal values. Behind a course on marriage there is bound to be some background, some faint survival of Puritanism; behind a course in government, the assumption that the "immortal principles" are an end. When the assumptions fail, much of the structure crumbles.

Myths are created, like that of the "economic man," by

those whose science, in itself, never permits getting out of the atmosphere, environment, and conventions of a time and place. In one room a professor settles the troublesome, subjective problem of value by defining it in quantitative, measurable terms as what most people want. Across the hall the professor of advertising shows that men don't know what they want, but must be told. For understanding the world we must have an historical sense, an awareness of the values of other countries and of other ages. This is an indispensable preparation precisely for the social sciences.

POSSIBILITIES AND ATTAINMENT

This account of the advantages of the study of foreign literature may not always correspond to the realities of the situation or to the experience of many who have studied the subject. Teachers often get lost in collateral interests or may never suspect what is involved in their duty. But the results outlined here are accomplished in many cases and could be, within the limits of the capacity of students, everywhere.

To eliminate study of foreign language and literature is to prescribe still more of the provincialism from which we suffer. Many need to be told that their home towns are not the centers of the world, but close to a cultural frontier. In America we build machines magnificently, but what we know about the refinements and elegances of life we must still largely import. We must attend the school of others, not merely for our own satisfaction, but to understand just where and how we are.

A responsible person would hesitate, one would think, to abolish a discipline which has formed the core of education for a thousand years, and which has helped to produce almost all the cultivated and distinguished minds we have had and nearly all our leaders, including even generals. Perhaps it was all a mistake; but the burden of proof is on those who wish to substitute their disciplines.

The reform of education probably does not lie so much in changes of subject matter as in changes in personnel, both in the faculties and in the student bodies. Time can cure many abuses, whereas those who, in their impatience, are always rushing for their guns seldom realize the utopias of which they dream. And in the meantime they upset everything, hurt themselves and others. This is true of political revolutions, and might be true of educational revolutions. It is conceivable, of course, that Time has been working, that modern language teachers have already been allowed to hang themselves. In that case, the efforts of sincere outsiders should be to save the values that have been neglected.

Part Three

METHODS, WORD COUNTS, TEXTBOOKS

V

The Battle of the Methods

METHODS ARE THE least important matter with which the language "methodologist" deals. This paradox is not hard to understand. The vital question is always the aim and the particular devices used to attain it, not generalized plans and philosophies. One might go still further and say that "methods" in the sense of *the* "Direct Method," *the* "Grammar Method," *the* "Natural Method," and so on, have no real existence. They are like *the* Frenchman (an abstraction) who has never been seen on land or sea. Just as Frenchmen exist in infinite concrete variations, some large, some small, some intelligent, some unintelligent, so it is with methods. When they become concrete and can be examined, they turn out to be this textbook or that.

It is sometimes convenient to speak of the "Direct Method" or the "Grammar Method" as an abstract classification of certain general procedures. But frequently a good deal of harm is done. Abstractions, since they are generally vague, arouse loyalties and emotions, so that discussion of them is transferred from a field of scientific investigation to a realm of feeling. It is easy to root for the Direct Method, whereas enthusiasm would be limited, if not entirely stopped, for Mr. Brown's or Mr. Smith's "Direct Method Applied."

Quarrels over method have divided teachers into hostile camps between which communication and mutual understanding are almost impossible. Everything here is vague and undefined. The professed common aim, accepted blithely and cavalierly, is usually to teach the foreign language. But what language, whose language?—the language of an academician or of a child? Every social class, profession, and trade has its own special vocabulary, metaphors, and usages. Moreover, what is *learning* a language? If it is learning absolutely, that is impossible, since no one knows French, English, or any other tongue in an absolute sense.

THE LIVING SPEECH

Certain unanalysed terms used in discussions seem to silence argument, for example, "living speech." Suppose you asked a group of high school pupils or their parents which they would prefer, a "living" speech or a "dead" language. The choice would hardly be doubtful. We all prefer what is living to what is dead. The terms "direct" and "natural" also have a certain force. Who does not prefer the direct to the indirect, the natural to the unnatural or artificial? In terminology, the direct methodists have had the best of it, since they started the fight and chose the words about which the battle would center and which would constitute a defense.

A certain romanticism in thought and expression has made the voice of common sense difficult to hear. The term "spoken language," for instance, is used like a bludgeon. Some maintain that language consists of sounds, not of symbols (signs), and that the literary language is always full of superfluous words and phrases that the common speech nearly always gets rid of. This is probably true. But

THE BATTLE OF THE METHODS

whose spoken language are they talking about, whose speech? And, in the case of the "living" tongue, what kind of life does it have? What is the nature of that life, and the value of it? Is not the speech of Virgil living after all these centuries quite as much as the speech of some contemporary mountaineer whose "living" speech dies in the ears of the few around him?

That the "living" speech consists of sounds, no one would dispute, nor that the written language consists of signs—but what of it? Are sounds more important than symbols? An overwhelming part of all the important communication in the world is in the form of books, newspapers, magazines, letters, treaties, constitutions, documents, and telegrams. As for the word "natural," no teaching is natural where pupils are herded into a room to think and to work against their inclinations. You might think a child could learn French the way a dog learns to chase squirrels. If there is anything more unnatural than for a child to learn a speech different from that of the group around him, it would be hard to find.[1]

EXPERIMENTS WITH METHODS

A few ambitious experimenters have tried to prove the advantages or disadvantages of the "Direct Method" by comparing results in different classes. But, since the method itself is an abstraction, the attempt is like trying to weigh a ghost. You cannot apply a theory or philosophy, but only an embodiment of a theory. Then the question arises as to whose embodiment, whose direct method is to be measured. You can always weigh the mnemonic advantage of a certain arrangement of words in a vocabulary in comparison with another arrangement, but it is impossible to measure in a single experiment a complexity of fifty or a hundred devices and to determine the share of each factor of a conception in the result.

In classroom experiments, the variables involved are infinitely complex. The textbook is only one bundle of factors in the total situation. Other things are important also, the hour of the class, the students' individual load of work, the temperament of the teacher, the presence of disturbing individuals, even the effect of the weather at the moment of the final test, and so on. Every characteristic of the individuals involved in the coöperation has an influence. Those who have conducted such experiments have paid homage to the scientific method without understanding, however, all its rigor.

METHODS AND OBJECTIVES

In dealing with "methods," everything is contingent. A plan good for one instructor is bad for another; a method good for one pupil may be poison to another. A good teacher with a poor method may do better than a poor teacher with a good method. The best teacher with the best method cannot succeed when pupils are unwilling to learn.

The problem could be put in another way, and we could affirm that all methods are good depending upon the criterion for judging them. The most disorganized, difficult, uninviting, and awkward presentation of material might be best for a certain kind of discipline, i.e., for enforcing docility, concentration, practice in overcoming difficulties, and for a Calvinistic mortification of the mind.

The vital question in any given situation is, first, what to do. The way to do it can be considered later. There should be no quarrels between methods that involve different purposes. In many circumstances it is important to learn a foreign tongue actively, and the best means to accomplish that end is almost certainly different from the best means to learn to read. A method adapted to the particular needs of a foreign country might be inappropriate in the United States.

The quarrel over methods involved mainly the old question of "speaking knowledge" versus "reading knowledge," the direct methodists emphasizing the first, the upholders of the various grammar methods, the second. This question has been settled to some extent, officially, by the Henmon, Mackensie, and Coleman reports, which have recommended a skill somewhat vaguely defined as "reading knowledge" as the principal and professed aim of required courses in public schools. This aim could be given precise definition by specifying a certain number of items in the word frequency and idiom lists for a given period of study. The problem then would be closely defined, and experimentation could determine the best means for presenting each part and kind of this material.

If this recommendation were rigorously followed, the foreign language problem, as far as American schools are concerned, would be greatly simplified. But there is still some confusion, since both methods have always claimed everything in sight, and many direct methodists maintain, while accepting the reading aim, that the best approach even to this goal is "through the ear," that is, through the spoken language.

ORAL METHODS IN THE CLASSROOM

Although in a few exceptional cases surprising results occur, the attempt to teach how to speak a foreign language in the classroom must usually meet with a very limited success. The maximum period of study for most students in secondary schools is two years. In that time a student receives about 180 hours of class instruction (eighteen ten-hour days). If each student were able to speak for two minutes each hour (which is more than is possible in most cases) the total amount of actual speaking would be 360 minutes, or about six hours.[2]

Many of the principles on which the Direct Method is based are probably quite correct as far as the spoken language is concerned. That "one learns to speak by speaking" is true to the extent that one can, under any system of class instruction, actually speak. The theory of the isolation of languages, the avoidance of interferences and associations due to the mother tongue, is also probably correct as a generalization. This isolation occurs at its best when a student goes to the foreign country and is cut off from his habitual speech. But in the beginning stages, as many have pointed out, the most extreme care to avoid the mother tongue cannot quite eliminate it. The child hears, for example, *das Schiff* many times; then, suddenly, in a flash, the meaning dawns: "Why, it's a boat!" he reflects.[3] This is inevitable.

The use of pictures, realia, gestures, etc., has no immediate advantage established experimentally except to maintain the integrity of a principle that cannot quite be lived up to. To develop every concept independently of its vernacular label would require reconstructing the pupil's mental life.

In America the majority of teachers are not equipped well enough to apply the direct methods, since they themselves can speak the foreign language only in an imperfect manner. To recommend better teachers might seem pertinent; but they can't be found, they don't exist. Many typical linguists are devoid of other talents or abilities.

The reliance upon concrete objects and upon actions

THE BATTLE OF THE METHODS 69

that can be demonstrated by gesture language, i.e., translated in that way, causes a curious limitation in the vocabulary used in the classroom. Everything connected with pens, pencils, notebooks, blackboards, etc., may be exhaustively covered, and relatively little else. The linguistic experience is limited to a childish sphere of interests.

The severest indictment of the oral methods lies, however, in what they attempt to do. The Berlitz schools are practical in their scope; they do not claim to educate in a broad sense, any more than schools where trades are taught, and their courses are not required of large sections of the population. Public schools, however, have other obligations. To consume time in teaching how to say what will never need to be said can be an abuse.

There are many apologies for the Direct Method, however. An intelligent teacher does good work in almost any situation, and there are intelligent teachers using all kinds of methods and textbooks. A skill not worth knowing taught by someone who knows it has still some advantages over such subjects as high school social science, about which the teacher herself may know very little.

In certain European schools where pupils begin their study of foreign languages young and continue them for many years, where there is a vital interest in the subject, the results of teaching by the direct methods have been eminently practical. It seems unfortunate, however, that a skill so difficult to acquire and so useless except in personal contacts with foreigners should require so much time. The practical skill does not measure all the gains, since oral methods, too, involve some reading of books and some broadening of experience. But the skill in itself must be paid for in time that might theoretically be used more profitably.

I believe that few people experienced in foreign language study would dissent seriously from the following recommendations for those who wish to learn to speak a foreign tongue. The list is in terms of first choice, second choice, and so on.

1. Go to the foreign country as young as possible and forget as far as you can your native language, or,

2. Learn to pronounce accurately by study and practice under competent guidance, then learn to read, then go abroad, or,

3. Substitute for going abroad in 2, living in a "French house" or "German house" in a college, or,

4. Take Berlitz or similar courses as long as you can.

A further option would be to give up the attempt.

THE GRAMMAR METHODS

The direct methods were a reaction against some of the abuses of the old grammar methods. The worst of these abuses were due to the assumption that grammar is the key to language knowledge. In a typical grammar method, rules were learned as a means by which *words* could be put together into phrases and sentences. If words were consistently the *units of expression,* the process might have been carried out, but, as will be shown, they are not.

The general aim of the grammar methods was vague or all-inclusive. The fundamental difference between reading knowledge and speaking knowledge was not recognized, or the two aims were confused. Students did acquire some reading ability, together with much mental discipline and drudgery, but it is doubtful if anyone ever learned to speak by rule.

The tenacity of these methods is explained in part by the satisfaction teachers gained in administering them. The instructors did not need to be fluent in the foreign tongue. They could compensate for this inferiority by knowing more rules of grammar than most of the millions of native speakers. The study was organized, moreover. It involved an intellectual discipline; it was not simply a matter of learning by heart, of knowing or not knowing, but there were reasons or pseudo-reasons for explaining everything. Thus the student could ask *why?* and the teacher triumph with a conclusive *because*. Explanations took up a large part of the class period, and a teacher who had explained clearly and efficiently *why* you say *DU sucre* or *LES chevaux sont DES animaux* could feel the satisfaction of work well done.

Under favorable circumstances all this could be quite interesting. It kept minds polished and working. It helped to develop intelligence, perhaps; it was dignified. It was concerned not with skills alone, but with principles behind the skills.

The only trouble is that language is not rational, that words are not necessarily significant linguistic units. Historical or morphological explanations can be given for linguistic phenomena, but the only logical reason for most expressions is that the present generation received them from parents, the parents from grandparents, and so on. All the rest may explain *how*, but not *why*, and the reasons, rules, categories, and principles of the treatises are so remote from the minds of those who speak the languages that they would be as surprised to hear of them as M. Jourdain was to learn that he spoke in prose.

The grammar taught, moreover, was of a peculiar sort. A French grammar for French boys is one thing, a grammar intended for English speaking pupils, quite another. A complete grammar, and none was ever complete, would have been a tremendous work. A general rule would appear, then a series of certain classes of exceptions, then exceptions within the exceptions, and conceivably exceptions within the exceptions to the exceptions. The situation might have been extremely grave except for a scrap heap on which were thrown the more remote exceptions: these were called "idioms." Sometimes a single idiom was of more frequent occurrence than a whole minor grammatical classification.

It was not fully realized that *comment allez-vous* is a unit, equivalent to "how do you do" in the same way that a single word, *chien* equals "dog." The student was supposed to go from one language to the other word by word, with the aid of rules and idioms. The process certainly gave the teacher something to think about and explain. How could the student know which words formed units or idioms and which did not, i.e., which could be taken separately? How could he know that *feu mon père* ("my late father") is not "fire my father," when *feu* means "fire," *mon* means "my," and *père* means "father." A whole is logically the sum of its parts—but not in language. In translating into the foreign tongue the student had no chance; he was trapped at every turn; each word and letter he put down was an opportunity for error. He was penalized for knowing a rule through forgetting an exception to it, and the rules were a complicated maze. The result was usually infinite practice in making errors. For learning to speak the language, the method was not quite, but almost, hopeless. Imagine the difficulties of a baby in learning to talk if he had to know that nouns are of several genders, that all *-tion* words are feminine, that the subjunctive occurs in certain adjectival clauses after various conjunctions and so on.

Grammar rules in this sense are a classification of cases, useful as a mnemonic aid when widely inclusive, but of value only for the economy of effort they may insure.

Conscious grammatical knowledge is so unimportant for the use of language that, at the time when Shakespeare, Milton, Dryden, Addison, Pope, and Johnson formed their style, there was no methodical treatise on the grammar of their native tongue in common use.[4] This is also true in respect to Cicero, Virgil, Horace, Pascal, and their contemporaries.

DEVICES OF THE GRAMMARIANS

The direct methodists rejected about every device that was used by the grammarians and, if you consider the spoken language alone, they were probably right. Whenever you want to develop skill in the spoken language, some procedures similar to those of the direct methods will probably prove most effective. But this does not mean that many of the devices used by grammarians would not still prove valuable in a method aimed primarily at reading knowledge.

The principal indictments have been directed against all translation, against paradigms, exercises composed of disconnected sentences or phrases, and, in general, against attempts to organize the material to be taught. To create the deep habits necessary for automatic speech, there must be infinite repetition of each phrase or of each type of phrase, and the order in which this material is presented (apart from considerations of frequency) is not important. The principal and most effective language teachers, i.e., mothers, have never followed a consciously organized plan. But the point to remember is that the mother's task does not go beyond speaking knowledge. For teaching a child how to read, she usually depends upon some tools or entrusts that task to others.

In the case of "translation," everything depends upon what is implied by the term. Translation may mean (1) going from the native to the foreign language, or (2) (a very different matter) going from the language being learned to the one already known. It may be considered (3) as a method for learning a foreign language, or (4) merely as a check on the student, a convenient test to enforce attention and understanding. Thus, it may be used to furnish practice in recall, as when a student covers up one column of words to test his ability to reproduce them and to sort out the known from the unknown items.

In the "natural," "oral," or "direct" methods for acquiring the spoken language, translation in any sense can have no important place. The aim in those methods is to separate the foreign medium as far as possible from the mother tongue. Still, a certain amount of translation occurs inevitably in the mind of the student, and there is no occasion to avoid it altogether as a test of knowledge, or to regard it on all occasions and in all forms with a kind of abhorrence.

VALUE OF TRANSLATION

As a test for a student's knowledge (to isolate one function only), nothing is more simple, direct, and convenient than translation. To a person knowing French and English, there is no difficulty at all in saying, for instance, that *Comment allez-vous* means "How do you do." No one with any competence at all would find in this a source of difficulty or confusion. It is the simplest and most natural thing in the world. It often happens, in dealing with fine distinctions and with experiences acquired in one lan-

THE BATTLE OF THE METHODS

guage and not in the other, that difficulty occurs, but that merely shows lack of balance between the two media.

It is understandable that students and those who pay more attention to sound than sense should disparage translation used in this way. It is a severe discipline, something rigorous, which permits almost no evasions, no escape. Students like to claim that they understand, but can't find the words to express their understanding. The truth, in almost all cases, is that their notion of the sense is a bit vague, and their inhibitions and difficulties a symptom of that vagueness. Try them on what you are sure they know, ask them what *chien* or *Hund* means and see how much confusion and difficulty they experience. This presupposes, of course, that the passage to be translated into the vernacular is reasonably simple in statement and clear.

Some things are not translatable, e.g., nonsense ("eenie, meenie, minie, mo"), trade names of articles that do not exist in the foreign country, many technical and scientific terms in fields that have not been developed at an equal pace in two countries, and anything which is beyond the depth of the reader because of his limited experience or immaturity, or because of the awkwardness and obscurity in the thought or style of the writer. In the case of lyric poetry, especially hypnotic verse, only the literal meaning as communication can be given, not the evocative value, which may be of most importance.

These limitations are very few. The one, outstanding, all-important fact is that you cannot translate what you do not understand. There are perhaps a few exceptions in the case of metaphysical or other cognates which are not understood in either tongue, but that is all. In so far as *understanding* is important, the process of translation from the unfamiliar to the familiar should be extended to all branches of study, and should constitute the fundamental and principal educational discipline. In English courses, for instance, there should be practice in translating euphemisms, emotive terms, figures of speech into plainer language, and statements of fact into terms of authority, motive, and the meaning that the laws of evidence permit.

As a method for learning to speak or write a language translation of connected passages from the vernacular into the foreign tongue probably deserves the abuse it has received. The process usually involves the fallacy that words can be put together with the aid of rules like digits in arithmetic. If vocabulary were expressed always in terms of *units of expression,* this arithmetical process might be possible, but in dealing with words, it affords mainly practice in making errors.

The English sentences used for translation exercises in the old grammars have frequently been parodied, as, for instance, "The merchant is swimming with (*avec*) the gardener's son, but the Dutchman has the fine gun."[5] The artificiality is obvious, but it is really not that which is ridiculous. The trouble is probably that the artificiality is not greater, or that it is given a semblance of naturalness. As an exercise in recall, the units might be presented as follows:

the merchant	*le marchand*
is-swimming	*nage*
with	*avec*
the son	*le fils*
of-the gardener	*du jardinier*
but	*mais*
the Dutchman	*le Holondais*
has	*a*
the fine gun	*le beau fusil*

THE BATTLE OF THE METHODS 77

Here what is ridiculous is the disorganization and disparity in the collection of items for recall, but even that might be, in some cases, excusable.

The abolition of all translation by many of the direct methodists led to certain practical difficulties. Mental translation occurred anyway and, without exercises in translation, it was difficult to enforce study, to give outside work a precise, definite, and easily measurable quality. The main dependence was on what the student was willing to pick up in class. The plan hardly fitted into a system of "studial" learning, and seemed to some critics easy and unintellectual. Since the amount of studial learning possible was limited, and since the attention of students wanders when not given a fixed task, the progress was generally slow.

When teaching an active use of a foreign language is justified, it is probable that something like the direct methods is the best means to accomplish this end. But in those cases where the main dependence must be on individual, independent study, the most effective means to enforce attention, to provide for practice, would still be to offer words or phrases for translation, or, to use a less confusing term, for practice in recall. But this can be done usefully only by eliminating the traps, pitfalls, tricks, and guides into error that the conventionally written vernacular contains. It will be necessary to present *units of expression,* to find typographical means to indicate what these units are, and where the traps lie.

Translation of natural, connected discourse or of passages from prose authors into a foreign tongue is almost impossible for a beginner, and should not be attempted. The ability to do this is an end-result, possible only when the two languages are well known. A very special mental process is involved. The expert translator ignores the words as they come, but thinks of the idea to be expressed, the idea as a whole. Then, re-thinking that idea in the foreign tongue, he expresses it in the conventions of that language.

Thus, with the phrase "The girl is running down the stairs," the whole action is thought of, and the expression of the idea comes in its French form as *"La petite fille descend l'escalier en courant."* The student who is learning the language cannot possibly know that the French think of the action in a slightly different form. He may start bravely with *"la petite fille."* Then he comes to "is running," which he recalls as the present tense of *courir*, i.e., "court." Later he sees that the verb is not "to run" but "to run down." If he doesn't notice this connection of *down* with the verb, he will write, *"La petite fille court bas l'escalier."* In any case, he would hardly suspect that in the French way of thinking "to run down" is "to descend in running." [6]

The rules and illustrations which are supposed to offer some help are almost infinite in number and are paralyzing in their effect. To guide the student through the pitfalls and chicaneries of this kind of translation, thousands of rules would need to be at his command.

If English is used in exercise material for studial learning, it should be merely for the purpose of designating certain French units of expression that the student should practice recalling, and these should be written with typographical devices to indicate clearly which units or which special locutions are involved. Used in this way, English phrases can facilitate the student's work of memorizing. They can be assigned as a task; they can enforce attention both at home and in class.

THE BATTLE OF THE METHODS

PARADIGMS, WORD LISTS, EXERCISES

In presenting phrases or units of expression only, a textbook writer would encounter a stubborn prejudice. The word has been passed around that word lists, phrases, and disconnected sentences are all objectionable. Why this idea has got abroad is hard to see, unless it was connected somehow with the realization that words as conventionally written and joined are treacherous. But, in the present recommendation, if single words appear, they will do so only as units of expression which by definition are capable of addition to or combination with other units. A child first begins to speak in single words. It is simply nonsense to suppose that a boy who has learned that "the girl" = *la petite fille,* "to run down something" = *descendre quelque chose en courant,* and "the stairs" = *l'escalier,* could not put these elements together and say, "*La petite fille descend l'escalier en courant.*"

It is precisely by means of such lists of units of expression that the presentation of material can be organized systematically and provision made for whatever economy in the learning process organization can insure. Connected discourse, on the other hand, introduces nouns, verbs, adjectives, pronouns, idioms, the important, the unimportant, in utter confusion. To orderly minds (and there are some even among students) this can only cause indigestion. Nothing is begun or ended; there is no chance to look back with satisfaction at work that has been completed; no sense of progress. *Vous avez* comes on one page, *ils ont* three pages later, *ayons* in a later chapter, so that if a student ever did know the verb *avoir* he would never know when he knew it. From the direct method viewpoint, which implies that every expression must have a deep and independent path in the brain, this disorganization does not matter, any more than it does in the haphazard teaching of a mother. But it is hard to conceive of many subjects being taught in that manner, especially those that demand independent study. It is an admission of helplessness on the part of the textbook writer.

The same objections have been made against paradigms, in the sacred name of "naturalness," as if that had anything to do with the matter. It ought to be possible to determine experimentally whether it is easier to learn groupings of related forms than mixtures. For recognition knowledge, the question is already answered. In any case, for the sake of orderliness alone, it would be better to arrange the material, in the same way that the multiplication table is organized.

THE DOCTRINE OF INTEREST

Another doctrine that has become widespread is that all the material presented to the student should be in an interesting form. Ergo, since a fairy tale is interesting to children who can read it easily and because they can read it easily, we should start students in high school or college who can't read at all with a fairy tale. Nothing is more pitiful than this logic which assumes that interest in one situation exists always and everywhere.

In learning a foreign language there is a vast amount of plain drudgery, i.e., memorizing: why should anyone fool himself? Incidental and effortless learning exists, but it has severe limitations. A few beliefs, such as "Smith is the people's choice" can be introduced painlessly into the mind by suggestion; also some words, but the process is slow and demands repetition over and over again. It is incompatible with studial learning. If the process were

THE BATTLE OF THE METHODS

generally applied, fifty years would not be enough to teach what is generally learned in four or five.

The commercial success of many recent language textbooks depends not on their efficient presentation of the work, but on the fact that classes in the public schools and colleges are becoming more and more filled with students who cannot or will not concentrate and for whom formal study is unprofitable. Nobody is urged by an eagerness to learn, and the most convenient and practical text is the one that enables the teacher to pass the hours and months most pleasantly. Some students pass through two years of French in high school and at the end of that time can hardly be trusted as a group to know thoroughly the definite and indefinite articles. This is certainly true of many rural high schools.

In textbooks planned consciously or not for killing time, there are few paradigms, many illustrations, much talk about the language, and nothing that looks hard. The grave problem of the French irregular verbs, without which nothing can be read or understood, is avoided as far as possible; the verbs are spread out, deferred, or even relegated to the appendix. So, likewise, the subjunctive, as if you could tell what you want in French without it. In many classes the medicine apparently must be administered in small doses and at long intervals.

But it is wrong to suppose that students hate work under all conditions. Work can be interesting, as every child who builds things knows. But students must understand what they are doing, and feel that they are getting somewhere. If it takes an hour with play and indirection to accomplish a certain task, and five minutes without the amusement, most students will prefer the second method. The problem of rapid and easy learning is to find means to insure brief moments of intense concentration. Only those who have seen what can be accomplished in time measured, not by minutes or hours, but by seconds will be in a position to understand this precept.[7] The question is really what kind of interest to arouse; and superficial appearances can never be trusted.

The old grammar methods were often a bore. The hopelessness of the tasks, the eternal affront of errors, the chicaneries, irrationalities, unless cleverly handled by the teacher, not only destroyed interest, but awakened a bitter hostility. The direct methods intended to correct all this by going to another extreme, and many teachers succeeded at once. Here was the living language, here was the chance to be able to order a *tête de veau* in an assured and casual manner. The instructor, either French or excessively *francisé*, also was interesting. No heavy books, no tables, formulas, problems, words to memorize, theories, equations! Instead, an entertainment, a show.

Yet every new wonder through constant familiarity becomes old and dull. The ingenuity of the instructor was taxed to provide entertainment as a performer that could be combined with any significant amount of hard work. Sometimes, because of the non-studial character of the discipline, two hours of conversation were equated in credit with one hour in the usual type of course—a matter that sometimes changed the rosy picture.

The compromise methods that have followed the warfare of the direct and grammar methods have combined frequently the worst features of both. The paradigms, word lists, careful organization are gone; likewise most of the entertainment. The compromises have had mainly the commercial advantage of not shocking widespread opinion. But the situation is not any better, and those who have no vested interest in foreign language study are beginning to regard the whole thing as a kind of waste.

NEW PROCEDURES

If reading knowledge alone becomes frankly and openly the aim of foreign language instruction in school, a new type of method, i.e., book, must appear. Fifteen years ago, or even ten years ago, there was not sufficient recognition of the profound difference between an active and a passive knowledge of a language, and even if it had been realized, the prestige of speaking was too great to permit entire candor. To ignore the spoken language seemed like putting French, German, and Spanish in the category of dead languages. But things have not worked out well, and all required language study is now being threatened.

To save the situation, the aims for the language courses should be clearer, and single, for each type of course. There might be courses in writing and speaking French, but the maximum *requirements* should involve reading knowledge only. Under favorable circumstances, the accomplishment of this last aim might be so rapid that present results would look pitiful.

Some writers, e.g., Michael West, maintain that for the majority of students the best means to attain a speaking knowledge is first through reading knowledge. The argument is plausible. When you can read a language with ease, you are close to a speaking knowledge. In any case, the reading objective is about the only one that can now be countenanced for all students, and it remains for textbook writers and teachers to show how efficiently that aim can be accomplished.

VI

Word Counts and Units of Expression

THE ERROR involved in word counts is what Palmer calls "the fallacy of the monolog," that is, the assumption that monologs alone have the right to be considered as units. The prefixes and suffixes (miologs) such as -less, dis-, re-, -like, -er, can be detached and placed in new combinations exactly in the same way as words. For example, "soulless," "shoeless," "subnormal," "substandard," "hatter," "armourer," etc.; likewise certain groups of words function as single words: "to take place," "to be in trouble," "to cause an effect," *avoir lieu, bon marché, comme il faut, vin à emporter, défense d'entrer, feuille de papier.*[1] "To take the bull by the horns" is usually a single verb which has nothing to do with actual bulls or horns. In the usual word counts, however, each word would count as a separate item. The word "bulls" would be included as in the phrase, "There are two bulls in the pasture."

But this is only part of the difficulty. Word counts list only the frequency of spellings, and ignore generally the semantic variations which are the most important matter, since obviously without knowing its meaning a word can neither be used nor understood. A few examples illustrate the multiplicity of meanings of single words. The adjective "hard," for instance, occurs in "hard-headed," "hard

WORD COUNTS AND UNITS OF EXPRESSION

of hearing," "a hard look," "a hard line," "a hard winter." In French, there are *cheveux blancs, viande blanche, la monnaie blanche, une arme blanche, un homme blanc, le pain blanc, une nuit blanche.* Nouns also vary in meaning according to the phrases in which they occur: *pied de giroflée, pied d'une montagne, pied d'une perpendiculaire, pied d'une marmite, pied-de-chat, pied de coq.*[2] You "take" a bath, you "take" the train, you "take" precautions, you "catch" a train, "catch" cold, you "close" a door, a road, an establishment, a debate, your ears, your mind and heart, quotations and parentheses. A single sentence will illustrate these semantic variations: "I don't *mind minding* the children, but they'll have to *mind, mind!*"[3] The word "get" has at least ten common semantic variations. Only one spelling is involved, but is "get" one word or ten? The German verb *halten* requires twenty-eight French verbs to express its meanings in various phrases. Ten semantic variations of a single spelling amount to ten different items, in the same way that a teamster's horse and a carpenter's horse are two different objects. To count spellings alone is certainly not enough.

In an experiment by Prof. E. L. Thorndike on the interpretation of shifts of function by a class of university students, 418 verbs used as nouns yielded 866 different meanings to the students, classifiable into 134 types, plus 158 figurative uses. One imaginary usage, employed in an experiment, was given 42 different meanings. Of twenty nouns used as verbs none would mean the same to fifty individuals.[4]

Still other difficulties arise. Are "I," "me," "we," and "us" one word or four? Are the hundred or so forms of each irregular French verb one item or separate items? There are perhaps a thousand inflected forms hidden in the first hundred items of the Van der Beke word count. A spelling occurring a hundred times in ten equally divided senses would be equal in value for any given meaning to another word with a frequency of only ten if this word were used in one sense only.

THE UNIT OF LANGUAGE

Before a science of language learning can be founded, a decision must be made as to what are the units of language. Grammars, dictionaries, and pedagogical works generally consider the word as the primary unit. The slightest consideration must show that this cannot be the case. And yet, except for the work of H. E. Palmer, little progress has been made in determining and designating any other units.

Early students of language reasoned as follows: A language is a collection of words joined together by certain principles or rules. The subject of language learning can be covered by collecting the words in dictionaries and the rules in grammars. The intricacies involved in this conception are as great as in the Ptolemaic cosmogony.

Words are, to use a phrase of Palmer's, nothing but "graphic accidents." In English, to quote Palmer further, we say "matchbox," but not "letterbox"; "teaspoon" but not "soupspoon"; "teapot," but not "coffeepot"; "gaslight," but not "gasfire"; "cannot," but not "mustnot"; "highways," but not "highseas." We say "yesterday" as one word; "to-day" and "to-morrow" sometimes as compounds; "last week" as two words. Likewise in French, you say *quoique* as one word, and its exact synonym *bien que* as two. In German you find such divisions as *gehe aus*, and *ausgehen*. Some words form compounds when closely related, while others do not. We have, for instance, "cupboard," "gentleman," "halfpenny," "sixpence," "altogether," etc., and, as two or more words, "all right," "of course," 'hardly ever," "scarcely any." Two or more words in English may stand for one in French, and vice versa: "hopeless," *sans espoir;* "typewriter," *machine à écrire;* "cherry tree," *cerisier.* And so on endlessly. There is no consistent rule as to what shall and what shall not constitute a word. "Motor car" started as two words and has lately become one. Certain syllables at one time were independent words, the word "manly" being, for instance, "man like," and "understand" a compound of "under" and "stand." Words like "cup board" passed through the hyphenated stage to "cupboard." [5]

It is hard to believe that units in language cannot be found, and yet none is perceptible at first sight. Words may be less than the unit or more than the unit. Some objects are designated by a single word whereas other similar objects are symbolized by several words. A dictionary definition is usually a series of words which taken together are equivalent to the monolog defined. When we don't know a name we paraphrase: metempsychosis, the-doctrine-of-the-transmigration-of-souls. The paraphrase is not a single word, but equivalent in function and use. Some monologs equal polylogs, and certain polylogs equal monologs. In *Bêche-de-mer,* for instance, the word piano is "big fellow bokus you fight him he cry"; a pregnant woman in this curious speech is "woman he got faminil inside." [6]

Just as a semantic unit may be represented by more than a word, a word may contain more than one semantic unit. Of the two elements in "hopeless," one is found separately in "hope," and the other in "formless," "guileless," etc., and the same is true of many other prefixes and suffixes.[7] To take a foreign example, Latin *amat* is really two words as is its English equivalent, the final "t" being originally a pronoun signifying "he," "she," or "it." The really essential difference between *amat* and "he loves" is that in the former the pronominal element is expressed by a suffix, in the latter by a prefix.[8]

Some words can stand alone in an enumeration and represent fairly definite concrete objects, e.g., "typewriter," "cherry," "football." Others summarize an experience that a book would be required to explain, e.g., "economic determinism," "evolution," "romanticism," "dialectical materialism." Others may express an entire wish, command, or warning: "Fire!" "Scram!" Some stand for actions, some for things, some for nothing concrete at all, e.g., "the ether," "Limbus," the "Fountain of Youth." Some express emotions, "ouch!," "liberty," "justice." Some vary in meaning with the tone of the voice: "Fine work!" And so on. Some stand neither for an object nor a sensation: "of," "from."

If this is not confusion, it is difficult to comprehend what confusion is.

What, then, do we organize in our speech? Is it syllables, words, groups of words, or sentences? Or are these merely artificial divisions which have no foundation in actual speech? An illiterate has no notion of the division of his speech into words.

The truth seems to be that the unit of language is sometimes less than a word, sometimes a word, sometimes a group of words, and sometimes what is graphically represented as a sentence. There are also pattern forms into which we fit individual words to suit the particular occasion. Individual style, as Michael West states, "depends upon the repertory of sentence forms and on the choice of favorites."[9]

By a unit is meant a group of syllables or of words that in a given usage is indivisible, and which can be combined, added or subtracted in sentences, paragraphs, and pages of connected discourse. No one doubts that units exist: otherwise we could hardly talk, since all speech is putting together links in a kind of chain. If the exact links were known, their frequencies established, then the order of learning would be definitely determined, and by experimentation the best means could be found for memorizing the list. Textbooks would no more differ in the order of presenting material than arithmetics, which must begin with the digits. Language learning would be reduced largely to memorizing the units of expression.

Speech can go on quite well, as it has been going on for centuries, without knowing what the *absolute* units are or how best to represent them. The absolute unit within a given language or in relation to all other languages is a psychological problem of tremendous difficulty. And if it is ever solved, there is no assurance that the knowledge would prove useful in learning a given foreign tongue.

But before a foreign language can be presented efficiently, the unit, at least in relation to the other tongue, must be known. When a student of French is taught the words for "father," "my," and "fire," he is not prepared at all for the unit *feu mon père* ("my late father"), and this difficulty is precisely one that introduces disorder, discourages the student, and makes an exact outline of the subject matter to be covered impossible.

If units relative to the language to be taught could be established, and if they formed the items of frequency counts, the basic problem of what to teach would be solved. At present this is known roughly, but not precisely. The deceptions and obscurities implied in taking words for units probably account for the failure to make more use of the frequency idea.

The relative units are obviously of various kinds. As already pointed out, in some cases they may be less than a word, in some cases more than a word. A word may constitute a unit in one connection and not in another. We are dealing with nothing fixed or settled, but with something constantly shifting. To perceive movement at all, it is necessary to establish a relationship or comparison, and another language can provide this, or rather can reveal the differences in shifts of meaning which, for the student of any particular tongue, are all that count. Thus the words "I-am-going," in such a sentence as "I am going to speak" might represent merely a future-tense ending in the case of a language not having the "am-going" future, but in relation to French the "I-am-going" could stand alone as a unit equaling *je vais*.

The following passage will help to illustrate the links that make up one language in comparison with another:

Pendant une belle matinée de printemps...la petite Marguerite...étant allée...se promener...se mit à cueillir ...des fleurs...dont elle voulait...se composer...un bouquet.

Au pied même...de la haie...la jeune fille...aperçut... des violettes...si nombreuses...si jolies...si odorantes... qu'enchantée de cette trouvaille inattendue...elle se disposa ...à les cueillir.

Comme elle s'approchait...toute radieuse...une vieille paysanne...s'écria: "Eloigne-toi...ma chère fille...de cette haie dangereuse. Des vipères malfaisantes et dangereuses... en ont fait...leur retraite.

Marguerite...naturellement timide et craintive...recula ...d'abord...épouvantée,...mais...le désir d'avoir...de

WORD COUNTS AND UNITS OF EXPRESSION 91

jolies fleurs...l'emporta...bientôt. Il me faut encore...se dit-elle...ces belles violettes...que j'aperçois...là-bas. Déjà ...la malheureuse petite fille...se baisse...pour mettre la main...sur son trésor,...mais...soudain...une hideuse vipère...s'élance sur elle...et lui fait une cruelle morsure.

Aux cris horribles poussés par l'enfant...la bonne femme ...va chercher...du secours. Quand le médecin arrive...il trouve...la pauvre Marguerite...tout à l'heure...si charmante et si gaie...déjà...froide et immobile...comme un cadavre. Heureusement...il peut lui administrer...des médicaments énergiques...qui la rappellent...bientôt ...à la vie. Mais...quelle cruelle et sévère leçon...elle a reçue...et...comme elle se promet bien...de n'oublier jamais...que l'on doit se modérer...dans ses désirs...même les plus simples et les plus inoffensifs...en apparence.

Leaving aside the matter of position and agreement, the groups of words which form units in the above passage can be classified as follows:

1. Type phrases in which other nouns, adjectives, etc., can be substituted. These phrases form patterns, and the pattern itself constitutes the unit. Ex., *la petite Marguerite (le gros Jean,* etc.); *être allée (arrivée,* etc.); *une matinée de printemps (un banc de pierre,* etc.); *étendre (montrer) la main (le pied,* etc.).

2. Combinations of words which do not equal the sum of their parts (counting only usual or conventional meanings); *le long de; se mettre à; il me faut; tout à l'heure,* etc.

3. Phrases involving words with variable meanings: *une petite fille, une jeune fille; pousser vite, pousser un cri,* etc.

The other units which require separate counting in frequency lists are words and parts of words, i.e., miologs (stems, endings, prefixes, and suffixes).

The frequency list of all items occurring more than once in the above passage is as follows:

-s (plu. of nouns and adjectives)	19
-e (fem. of adjectives and past part.)	13
et, and	8
elle, she, it, her	7
-se (adj. fem. ending)	7
-t (pres. and past abs. verb ending)	7
la (l'), the	6
-e (pres. and imperative verb ending)	6
de, of, from	5
si, so	5
des, some	4
-é (verb ending, past part.)	4
-er (infinitive ending)	4
une, a, an (one)	3
le (l'), the	3
les, the	3
haie, hedge	3
-a (verb ending, past abs.)	3
se (reflexive pro.)	3
que (qu'), that, which, whom	3
mais, but	3
un, a, an (one)	2
de, some	2
de (functional only)	2
à, to, at	2
la (l'), her, it	2
il, he, it	2
-ait (verb ending, imperf.)	2
-ir (verb ending, inf.)	2
-ment (adv. suffix)	2
bientôt, soon	2

WORD COUNTS AND UNITS OF EXPRESSION

déjà, already	2
plus, more, most	2
cueill- (verb stem)	2
son, his, her, its, one's	2
belle, fine, beautiful	2
petit, little, small	2
cette, this, that	2
dangereu- (adj. stem)	2
cruelle, cruel	2
violette, violet	2
vipère, viper	2
in- (prefix)	2
la petite Marguerite, (phrase pattern)	2

This kind of frequency count bears little resemblance to those in current use. It has many advantages. It separates the semantic variations. The word *même*, for instance, occurs three times in the above passage with three different meanings, "same," "very," and "even." From every viewpoint, especially that of learning, this common spelling represents three words that deserve to be counted separately.

Except for the matter of word order and rules for agreement, the above type of frequency count indicates all the subject matter to be taught and the relative importance of that subject matter. The verb stems and endings are certainly part of the learning problem. A verb like *avoir,* for instance, if presented as a single item, is full of deceptions, because *ont, eu, eussions*, etc., are discreetly hidden. On the other hand, if all the hundred or so forms were presented, the learning problem would be similarly disguised, since the problem is not nearly so difficult as that. Miologs are as real as anything in the language. We add endings to new verbs we have never used before as naturally as we join words together in our sentences. This count illustrates also the distribution of the tenses and offers a form for an almost complete outline of the subject matter.

The units composed of more than one word are also included, as they should be. In the case of *se promener* we are dealing with a single unit which, as far as the generalized form is concerned, might be written *sepromener*, "to-take-a-walk." In *se laver*, however, we are dealing with two separate units, in relation to English, "to-wash" and "oneself."

Typographical devices are needed to point out the units and to make the student conscious of them. Perhaps the best method of all is precisely to present short phrases in columns, as shown above. These indicate clearly what words go together, and establish the necessary associations. They also reveal the word order, and by appearing in columns allow for checking of knowledge and efficient study. Phrases for practice should be in generalized form, however, whenever possible, e.g., *faire faire quelque chose* to "have" something "made" ("done"), not, *Jean s'est fait faire un complet*, except as an illustration under the generalized form.

It is unfortunate that a plan of this kind was not made before the present word and idiom counts were started; but that fact does not detract from the merit of the intention. The present counts are not old, and yet they were, in a way, pioneering efforts. They are still a helpful guide, and by various samplings of meanings and study of single items it might be possible to correct and combine the lists and to add to them the items such as miologs that were omitted entirely. We would have then an exact outline of the work to be accomplished, i.e., an exact idea of what to teach.

VII

Textbooks in Foreign Languages

IN SOME subjects a textbook is not indispensable and must be supplemented by the teacher's efforts or by outside reading. In language study the textbook is, or should be, everything. There is here little occasion for qualifications, opinions, or taste. A word usually is spelled one way and one way only; a tense is past or present, and so on. There should be little variation in content of beginning texts intended for a particular purpose, and the memorizing involved is a mechanical process which requires no great amount of thought, originality, or critical spirit.

If this is true, methodology concerns principally writers of texts. No teacher can hope by purely extemporaneous improvisations to think up better illustrations or examples than he or she could deliberately work out. The textbook should be a tool not likely to be improved by casual efforts. When prepared properly it should be treated "with the same respectful non-interference we accord to the magnetos of our motor cars."[1] Progress in language teaching depends largely upon the books used.

As long as there is a multiplicity of aims in the same course, really effective texts will be hard to find. An effective tool can hardly be prepared for accomplishing something not clearly defined. But if the reading aim becomes definitely established in required school courses and if that ability is conceived in terms of a fixed list of words and phrases, the problem becomes relatively clear and simple. The textbook writer knowing what to present and having a criterion for measuring the value of his arrangements, i.e., economy of effort, can use all his ingenuity with the single aim of effecting this economy. Textbooks in this field should set a standard for presentation of material for memorization that could serve as a guide for the presentation of similar material in other fields.

In the last twenty years, however, there has been almost complete anarchy in the foreign language textbook field. Everyone has been bewildered by conflicting aims, and there has been no common understanding of the task. The rigorous direct method texts have been compromised for the sake of expediency as the cause of the direct methods failed to gain, and the old grammar methods, suffering from the deadly scorn of the direct methodists, had to disguise themselves as well. The compromises have often incorporated the confusion.

THE PUBLISHING BUSINESS

Some of the most unfortunate compromises have been encouraged by the textbook "business."

The system of publishing school books in the United States offers considerable liberty to authors and abundant opportunities. But commercialism, although not so rampant as in other businesses, is demanded here also by self-preservation. If a commercially successful book appears, the leading publishers come out with competing goods, just as any theme handled successfully in the movies leads to a series of more and more sickly imitations. Often competing editions are as alike as peas.

There would be no harm in this if successful books were necessarily good, but this is often not the case. Success here, as in popular writing, depends upon hitting the "middle of the market." The commercially successful books are not those that appeal to responsible experts, but rather those that fit in with the passing notions, principles, and dogmas of an academic mediocrity. In the United States where teachers of elementary courses are often young and bewildered, the center of the market is frequently deplorable. The most responsible men in the profession frequently consider elementary teaching as a bit of unimportant drudgery and would disdain even to read a treatise on the subject. Sometimes a book succeeds not because it helps the student in his task, but because it makes real learning unnecessary and helps by means of evasions to make the class hour pass easily and without strain. Real results in schools do not always count. If the teacher is cooperative, morally sound, pleasant to superiors, a good disciplinarian and not too unpopular with his or her charges, it matters little in the general scheme of things whether the pupils really learn or not. No minds are strained, no big or little children are worried or harassed.

The ballyhoo for textbooks is less blatant than for most commercial products; but publishers must compete with each other and sell to survive. Many procedures having no basis in experiment or in reason are presented as the final, i.e., latest, thing. Not to follow them is to be accused of being behind the times, of not doing (as in matters of etiquette) what is being done by those who do what is being done. At best mediocrity is pampered and exalted, as in the case of popular literature.

There is something almost sacred about a textbook. It should be prepared with a professional conscience, like holy water or sacramental food. In many matters, mistakes of fact or judgment are not important, but in textbooks the damage is multiplied, magnified enormously. As H. G. Wells has remarked, "a slip or obscurity which wastes five minutes, wastes ten or twenty or thirty thousand times five minutes of the nation's time." [2] A child may spend as much as fifty hours a month in the company of a textbook designed uniquely to sell and exploit some passing notion.

The French logical mind is a great help in preparing orderly texts, and the books used in France are under responsible control. Defects in our American minds as well as in our society would seem to demand constant and critical watchfulness. In America, because of a dominant commercialism, quackery is a greater danger than almost anywhere else.

EXPERIMENTATION

If the recommendations made at present concerning the scope of the foreign language work in required courses are widely accepted, the textbook problem could be solved experimentally. The material to be presented is not quite, but almost, established. The remaining problem is to discover by what means this material can be taught with the greatest economy of effort. There can be no testing, of course, of an entire book, but, in the case of each kind of material, the particular arrangements used in presenting it can be compared with other arrangements. Ultimately, not as the result of any individual's inspiration, but through a coöperative effort, a kind of technology could be developed, and the ultimate textbook would have the testing and experimentation behind it that mechanical structures have.

Here is a task for Schools of Education to take up. With

a definite solvable problem before them, and with their interest in testing, they could make important contributions to the technique of presenting verbal material for memorization. That would be better than studying memory in the abstract and remaining in the clouds. Some of the problems involve the advantage of grouping words by parts of speech, difficulty, and associations; the advantage of certain typographical devices as compared with others; printing phrases in columns versus setting solid, and so on; also the value of suggested associations, the arrangements and simplifications of verb paradigms, the handling of words that have numerous semantic variations, etc. The experiments could deal with actual materials, thus eliminating to a large extent the need for dangerous generalizations.

If this were done, the teacher's task would be simplified enormously, and the "teacher problem" made less serious. No special talents would be required other than those needed for teaching geography, arithmetic, or spelling. When emphasis is placed on the spoken language, many teachers not fluent in the foreign tongue, but of good mind and sufficiently ahead of their students, have feelings of inferiority. Their general abilities, which may be of a high order, are of little help to them. In some small high schools, it is frequently necessary to draft someone to teach French or German. Under these conditions all language study and teaching have suffered.

Part Four

SUGGESTIONS FOR A SCIENTIFIC METHOD
OF LANGUAGE TEACHING

VIII

A Plan for Teaching How to Read

IF READING KNOWLEDGE ALONE is to be required in public schools, most of the basic textbooks in current use will have to be changed, since nearly all of them compromise with the quite separate aims of teaching how to write and how to speak. The waste in doing this is too great and too obvious. In order to write or to speak French, for instance, one must know the gender of all the nouns used; merely to read, that knowledge is superfluous. It is enough to know, for example, that *le, l', la,* and *les* all mean "the," that *fourmi* means "ant," and *radio,* "radio," regardless of the genders of those words.

Most of the complicated rules for explaining how to transfer an English expression into French can be dispensed with. Problems of agreement, of prepositions with the infinitive, and so on, cease to be a vital matter, and entire emphasis can be placed on memorizing the units of expression in order of their frequency.

INFLECTED FORMS

Most of the inflected forms might, conceivably, be treated as any other items of a vocabulary, and in that case would appear in the order of their frequency, but, because of their unusual importance and difficulty, it would probably be better to present them together, systematically, in a special introduction.

The advantage of organization of material can be decided experimentally, but it would seem *a priori* that the memory task would certainly be lightened by some arrangements of the material, because of the pattern into which most of the forms fall and because meanings can be learned in a collective way, not entirely as separate items. Thus *mon, ton, son,* etc. should probably be treated together, not separately according to their chance occurrence in a strict frequency count. And so likewise with the other inflected forms.

A further advantage of organization is that it permits taking up one subject at a time and really completing it. This gives the student a sense of accomplishment, and he can realize what progress he is making. Nothing is more distracting than to give *vous allez* in one lesson, *ils vont* three or four lessons farther on, and so on. That practice is especially bad since the difficulty of learning words in combination with other words increases tremendously over the difficulty of learning the items separately.

VERB FORMS

Irregular verbs are the *bête noire* of most students. Many textbooks, through a confusion in aims, spread these verbs over a hundred pages or so, neglect certain necessary tenses, and even relegate some forms to the appendix. The present tense of one verb may be given in one lesson, the future several lessons farther on, the subjunctive at the end of the book. This prevents concentration on a single definite task, a feeling of finishing a well-defined part of the work. The apology may be that verbs are hard and must be given in small doses, and, if possible, surreptitiously. There is no surreptitious learning of verb forms, however: the learning must be conscious or there is no learning at all.

The first point to understand is that there can be no avoidance of the irregular verbs. They occur in the simplest, most colloquial speech. They are everywhere, on every page, in every paragraph, in nearly every line. Some single verbs, e.g., *aller* (certainly *avoir* and *être*) are more important than the entire third regular conjugation. These words form the core of the language, and without knowing them no reading of connected discourse is possible at all. There are about forty common irregular verbs in French. These occur about as frequently as all the thousands of regular verbs put together.

Irregular verbs are not nearly so difficult as generally supposed. If only the irregularities of stems and endings are shown and recognition knowledge alone is aimed at, the task of the verbs is greatly simplified. With college students, an ability to identify all the forms of the regular and irregular French verbs should be possible after a few hours of study, provided, of course, the presentation of these forms is organized and simplified.

PREPOSITIONS

Prepositions can hardly fail to be included with the inflected forms, since, although they are not inflected, practice phrases can hardly be composed without them, and many of them are among the words of highest frequency in the language.

The textbook writer should point out constantly that the common prepositions *à, de, par, pour, en,* etc., are functional words, that they have no fixed English equivalents (although some equivalents may fit more often than others), and that in varying situations they may be replaced by almost any English preposition. If this fact is thoroughly understood, perhaps half of the idiomatic phrases cease to be idiomatic and can be translated into English without difficulty.

In addition to the inflected forms proper and the prepositions, a number of common indefinite pronouns, adverbs, and conjunctions should also be included. They are not numerous, are needed in exercise material, and deserve first attention because of their high frequency of occurrence.

TABLE OF INFLECTED FORMS

ARTICLES: le, la, l', les; un, une.

POSSESSIVE ADJECTIVES AND PRONOUNS: mon, ma, mes; ton, ta, tes; son, sa, ses; notre, nos; votre, vos; leur, leurs; le mien, la mienne; le tien, la tienne; le sien, la sienne; le (la, les) nôtre (s); le (la, les) vôtre (s); le (la, les) leur (s).

DEMONSTRATIVE AND INTERROGATIVE ADJECTIVES AND PRONOUNS: ce, cet, cette, ces; quel, quelle; celui, celle, ceux; lequel, laquelle, lesquels, lesquelles; (miologs) -ci, -là.

CONTRACTED FORMS: du, au, des, aux; auquel, auxquels, auxquelles; duquel, desquels, desquelles.

PRONOUNS: je, moi, tu, toi, il, lui, elle, on, soi, nous, vous, ils, eux, me, te, se, leur, le, l', la, les, y, en.

REGULAR VERB ENDINGS: -er, -ir, -re, -ant, -é, -i, -u, -e, -es, -ent, -ons, -ez, -s, -t, -ions, -iez, -ais, -ait, -aient, -ai, -as, -a, -ont, -âmes, âtes, -èrent, -is, -it, îmes, -îtes, -irent, -asse, -asses, -ît, -assions, -assiez, -assent, -isse, -isses, -issions, -issiez.

IRREGULAR VERB ENDINGS: ai, as, a, ont, suis, es, est, sommes, êtes, sont, vais, vas, va, vont, faites, font, dites, peux, veux, vaux.

VERB STEMS: (donner) donn-; (finir) finiss-, fini-; (rompre) romp-, (rompu) romp-; (avoir) aur-, ay-, av-, ai-, (eu) eu-; (être) ser-, ét-, soi-, soy-, (été) fu-; (aller) ir-, all-, aill-; (as-

A PLAN FOR TEACHING HOW TO READ 107

seoir) asseyer-, assey-, assoy-, assied-, assoi-, (assis) assi-; (battre) batt-, bat-; boire, boi-, buv- (bu) bu-; (conduire) conduis-, condui- (conduit) conduisi-; (courir) courr-; (craindre) craign-, crain-, (craint) craigni-; (croire) croy-, croi-, cru-; (devoir) devr-, dev-, doi-, doiv-, (dû) du-; (dire) dis-, di-, (dit); (écrire) écriv-, écri-, (écrit) écrivi-; (envoyer) enverr-, envoi-, envoy-; (faire) fer-, fais-, fai-, fass-, (fait) fi-; (falloir) faudr-, fall-, fau- (fallu) fall- faill-; (lire) lis-, li-, lu-; (mettre) mett-, met, (mis) mi-; (mourir) mourr-, mour-, meur-, (mort) mouru-; (naître) naiss-, nai-, (né) naqui-; (ouvrir) ouvr-, (ouvert) ouvri-; (paraître) paraiss-, parai-, paru-; (plaire) plais-, plai-, plu-; (pouvoir) pourr-, pouv-, pui-, peuv-, puiss-, (pu) pu-; (prendre) pren-, prend-, prenn-, (pris) pri-; (recevoir) recevr-, recev-, reçoi-, reçoiv-, (reçu) reçu-; (savoir) saur-, sach-, sav-, sai-, (su) su-; (sentir) sent-, sen-; (suivre) suiv-, sui-; (venir) viendr-, ven-, vien-, vienn-, (venu) vin-; (valoir) vaudr-, val-, vau-, vaill-, (valu) valu-; (vivre) viv-, vi-, (vécu) vécu-; (voir) verr-, voy-, voi-, (vu) vi-; (vouloir) voudr-, voul-, veu-, veul-, veuill-, (voulu) voulu-.

PREPOSITIONS, ETC.: à, de, par, comme, pour, sur, en, dans, autour de, pendant, au-dessus de, au-dessous de, avant, après, chez; qui, que (qu'), dont; car, mais, et, si ou; ne ... pas, point, rien, guère, plus, jamais, que; aussi, d'abord, puis, plus, même, non, donc, encore, toujours, tout, tous, peu, enfin, bien, très, où, plusieurs, presque, mal, ainsi, bientôt, beaucoup, mieux, maintenant; re-, ra-, -ment.

This is a mere outline and suggestion. A few verb forms have been omitted (orthographical changes) and a few, but very few, other details. Some explanation would be necessary in connection with the verb forms, the formation of plurals, position of pronouns and negative expressions, etc., but the amount of this explanation could be very small.

The first problem of the textbook writer is to experiment to see in which ways this crude material can be arranged most effectively for learning and what exercises could insure effective study habits.

The material outlined above is considerable in amount, but in comparison with a grammar of several hundred pages, it is hardly anything at all. It would be interesting to see just how much French can be read with this material alone, which contains no nouns, adjectives, or regular verbs (except model forms). I have chosen at random two passages, one of what might be called "scientific French," the other of more elementary narrative character. A dialogue would give a higher percentage of irregular verbs and other inflected forms, but the material chosen fits in better with what is most apt to be read in school.

The first passage will be presented first in French, then transcribed, giving the English equivalents for (1) all the words included above; (2) those that appear a second time; and (3) those which would almost certainly be identified by any student for whom the passage would be appropriate:

Nous avons vu au livre I que le mouvement des étoiles par rapport à la terre, était un mouvement d'ensemble dû à la rotation de la sphère céleste autour de son axe. Le mouvement des autres astres que nous avons à étudier n'est pas aussi simple: nous nous occuperons d'abord du soleil. Le soleil participe au mouvement diurne; car, comme les étoiles à Paris, par exemple, il se lève chaque jour du côté de l'orient, s'élève à une certaine hauteur au-dessus de l'horizon, puis se couche du côté de l'oc-

We have seen in the *livre* I that the movement of the *étoiles* in *rapport* to the *terre* was a movement d'*ensemble,* due to the rotation of the celestial sphere around its axis. The movement of the *autres astres* that we have to *étudier* is not as simple. We will occupy (concern) ourselves first with the *soleil*. The sun participates in the diurnal movement; for, like the stars at Paris, for example, it *se lève chaque jour* in the *côté* of the east, rises to a certain *hauteur* above the horizon, then *se couche* in the direc-

A PLAN FOR TEACHING HOW TO READ 109

cident; mais les observations les plus simples suffisent pour montrer que le soleil ne reste pas fixe sur la sphère céleste, c'est-à-dire fixe par rapport aux étoiles. En effet, contrairement aux étoiles, le soleil ne se lève pas tous les jours au même point de l'horizon, et il ne s'élève pas non plus à une hauteur maxima constante au-dessus de l'horizon; il n'a donc pas, comme les étoiles, une déclinaison constante, ce qu'on exprime en disant qu'il a un mouvement propre en déclinaison.

Si l'on observe encore les constellations qui se lèvent ou se couchent peu de temps avant le lever ou après le coucher du soleil, on constate que ces constellations ne sont pas toujours les mêmes; dans le courant d'une année, par exemple, à partir de la fin de mai, on verra successivement le lever du soleil suivre de peu de temps le lever du Bélier ...etc.; puis, les mêmes phénomènes se reproduisent dans le même ordre les années suivantes. Comme les ascensions droites de ces constellations vont constamment en augmentant, il en résulte que le soleil a un mouvement propre en ascension droite, dans le sens des ascensions droites croissantes, c'est-à-dire dans le sens direct, inverse de celui du mouvement diurne, de l'ouest à l'est. Enfin, on peut aisément constater à chaque instant le mouvement propre du soleil sur

tion of the west; but the most simple observations suffice to show that the sun does not rest (remain) fixed on the celestial sphere, that is to say, fixed in relation to the stars. In *effet,* contrary to the stars, the sun does not rise all the days at the *même* point of the horizon, and it does not rise *non plus* to a constant maximum height above the horizon; it does not have then, like the stars, a constant declination, which one *exprime* by saying that it has a movement *propre* in declination.

If one observes further the constellations which rise or set a little time before the rise or after the setting of the sun, one *constate* that these constellations are not always the same; in the *courant* of a *année,* for example, *à partir de* the *fin* of May, one will see successively the rise of the sun follow by little *temps* the rise of the Bélier...etc.; then the same phenomena are reproduced in the same order the following years. As the ascensions *droites* of these constellations go constantly increasing, it results (turns out) that the sun has a movement of its own in right ascension, in the sense of right ascensions *croissantes,* that is to say, in the direct sense, the inverse of that of the diurnal movement, from west to east. Finally, one can easily note at each instant the movement of its own of the sun against the celes-

la sphère céleste de la façon suivante; supposons que l'on dirige sur le soleil la lunette d'un équatorial entraîné par un mouvement d'horlogerie suivant les lois du mouvement diurne; si le soleil était fixe sur la sphère céleste, il apparaîtrait fixe dans le champ de la lunette; au contraire, on voit l'image du soleil se déplacer lentement dans le champ de l'instrument.

tial sphere in the following *façon:* let us suppose that one *dirige* at the sun the *lunette* of an equatorial *entraînée* by a movement d'*horlogerie* following the laws of the diurnal movement; if the sun were fixed on the celestial sphere, it would appear fixed in the *champ* of the glass; on the contrary, one sees the image of the sun displaced *lentement* in the field of the instrument.

Without being a Champollion, it would not take a student who knew astronomy many days to work out this passage without any further help than the handful of forms that has been given above, and, if this were the test, a graduate student with a dictionary could pass his reading knowledge examination without knowing beforehand a single noun, regular verb, or adjective.

The second passage, although intended for younger readers, contains a still larger vocabulary. The items not included in the plan above will appear in italics.

Une *maîtresse* de *maison,* qui ne *surveillait* pas suffisament ses domestiques, voyait son *aisance* diminuer chaque année. Elle résolut d'aller consulter un *vieillard renommé* pour son expérience et sa *sagesse.* "Mon *père,* lui dit-elle, mon *ménage* ne va pas bien, mes affaires sont dans une très *mauvaise* situation. Indiquez-moi un remède à tous mes *maux.*

Le vieillard, qui était d'une humeur joviale, lui présenta une *petite cassette* bien *fermée,* en disant: "Pendant toute une *année,* vous *porterez* cette cassette, à la *cuisine,* à la cave, dans les *écuries,* les *granges,* dans les *bergeries,* enfin dans tous les *coins* et *recoins* de votre maison, *trois fois* par *jour* et trois fois par *nuit,* et je vous promets que l'aisance reviendra dans votre

A PLAN FOR TEACHING HOW TO READ

maison. Au *bout* de l'année n'*oubliez* pas de me rapporter la cassette."

La *bonne dame* qui avait une entière confiance dans l'efficacité de la cassette mystérieuse, suivit les recommandations du vieillard. Elle *promena* régulièrement ce coffret dans toutes les parties de sa maison. La *première* fois qu'elle descendit à la cave, elle y surprit le *garçon* d'écurie au moment où il *dérobait* plusieurs *bouteilles* de vin. Visitant la cuisine à une heure très avancée de la nuit, elle y *trouva* les servantes se *chauffant* autour d'un bon *feu* et se *régalant* de *friandises*. En entrant dans une des granges, elle s'*aperçut* que la *porte* en avait été *laissée* ouverte, que les *poules,* les *dindons,* les *oies* y avaient pénétré et y commettaient des dégâts. En *parcourant* les écuries, elle y vit les vaches presque *enterrées* dans une *litière infecte,* les *chevaux à jeun* et mal *soignés*. C'est ainsi qu'à toute heure elle avait à *réprimer* de *nouveaux* abus. La prospérité revint bientôt à la ferme, et la fermière, très superstitieuse, attribuait ce bienfait aux vertus de la cassette.

Au bout de l'année, l'excellente fermière reporta la cassette au vieillard, et l'*abordant* avec une *mine* joyeuse et *reconnaissante:* "Tout va beaucoup mieux chez moi maintenant, lui dit-elle; mais j'ai une prière à vous adresser: il faut que vous me laissiez encore la cassette pendant toute la nouvelle année."

Le vieillard lui répliqua: "Vous *céder* de nouveau ma précieuse cassette! non, je ne le ferai point; mais je vous ferai présent du remède qu'elle contient." Ce disant, le bon *solitaire* ouvrit la mystérieuse cassette. Qui fut bien surprise? Ce fut la bonne fermière, car elle n'y vit qu'une petite bande de papier sur laquelle on lisait ces *paroles:* "Il n'est, pour voir, que l'*oeil* du maître; c'est lui l'*homme* aux cent yeux, qui, ne laissant rien *échapper, veille* à ce que tout s'exécute bien dans la maison."

Those interested in statistics can figure out the proportion of unknown to known items, the relative number of regular and irregular verbs, the number of nouns that occur in both passages, and so on. The purpose here is only to illustrate the importance of the words grouped under the inflected forms.

It is worth noting, however, that of the nouns in the two passages not immediately recognizable, only two out of sixty-six are common to both passages; of twenty-nine verbs not included with the inflected forms, not one is common to both passages, and only one adjective out of nineteen. These words exist in almost endless succession; they are different for every subject or experience treated, and vary to some extent with every author.

VOCABULARY

In the outline of material given above no regular verbs, adjectives, or nouns have been included. It would be interesting to see what results in reading knowledge could come by adding to the list of forms given the words not already included which fall within the first 500 items in order of frequency.

This list can be reduced first by excluding those words exactly like their English cognates or which could hardly fail to be recognized in context, e.g., *doute, arriver, entrer, moment, toucher, revenir, remettre, relever*, etc. The remaining words can be grouped into three classes: (1) those relatively easy because of sound association, e.g., *temps*, time; *heure*, hour; etc., (2) those with logical associations, e.g., *dent* [dentist] tooth; *soleil* [solar] sun; *jour* [journal] day; *voici* [*vois ici*] here is, here are, etc., and (3) difficult words.

With a little training in the technique of association as a memory aid or by suggesting the associations, the words of the second group offer almost no difficulty at

A PLAN FOR TEACHING HOW TO READ

all. In an experiment with artificial material, it was found that average subjects could learn the devised meanings of 36 words for recall after 24 hours in nine minutes total time. At this rate the entire list in group 2 below could be learned in about half an hour of concentration, although the task would need to be distributed over many brief periods. The words in Group 1 are still easier.

The list of these words follows. The groupings are necessarily arbitrary in the case of particular items, but the general distinction is clear and evident.

1. Words with sound associations:

   autre, beau, temps, heure, laisser, nom, comprendre, sembler, vue, répondre, pauvre, milieu, haut, partir, état, monter, apercevoir, reconnaître, diriger, garder, juste, vérité, entier, coûter, étonner, cas, cour, pousser, étranger, cesser, français, prix, conseil, voix, marquer, papier, achever, prier, choisir, tour, gagner, expliquer, rentrer, histoire, quitter, compte maître, façon

2. Words with logical associations:

   bon, enfant, grand, femme, homme, jour, petit, tenir, entre, seul, moins, porter, place, vie, rester, an, nouveau, part, appeler, montrer, demander, parler, trois, sortir, fort, tomber, premier, sous, contre, seulement, vrai, main, attendre, perdre, aujourd'hui penser, pendant, fond, matin, terre, longtemps, esprit, argent, ami, nuit, plein, chercher, quatre, année, monde, aimer, maison, oublier, apprendre, apporter, mesure, dame, porte, cent, gens, ancien, fin, père, pied, tard, côté, fille, dieu, jeter, corps, surtout, élever, tendre (v.), mal (n.), quelqu'un, bras, parole, pareil, s'arrêter, lever, bas, gros, rencontrer, essayer, regarder, rappeler, manger, voici, grave, figure, libre, blanc, mort (n.), amour, poser, rouge, traverser, bord, coeur, ville, affaire, fils, regard, route, campagne, profond, emporter, large, convenir, ciel, soleil, occasion, mère, guerre, vif, vive, livre, pensée, journée, front deviner, dur, bas (n.), remarquer, doigt, vent.

3. Difficult words:
avec, deux, sans, tout, quelque, alors, chose, fois, jusqu'à, devenir, quand, même, (adv.), depuis, assez entendre, loin, trouver, cela, là, devant, peut-être, souvent, trop, tête, lieu, tirer, mot, lorsque, chaque, aucun, cependant, tant, peine, même (adj.), oeil, yeux, déjà, coup, cinq, besoin, vers, puisque, pourquoi, ici, pays, travail, jouer, malgré, mois, moyen, derrière, parce que, pourtant, droit (n.), bout, d'ailleurs, soir, tel, propre, comment, quoi, grâce, empêcher, parmi, charger, vieux, heureux, ajouter, songer, mauvais, ensemble, suite, voisin, tout (adv.), près de, jeune, bois, chacun, dès, cher, mille, huit, tandis que, vingt, bruit, meilleur, dehors, remplir, dix, fermer, mener, monsieur, âme, chemin, droit (adj.), sept, jusque, dernier, feu, doux, douce, ensuite, autant, vite, jambe, oui, ni, écouter, pleurer, espérer, demi, quinze, couper, siècle, soir, pas (n.), fait (n.) oser, semaine, frapper, guère, ailleurs fenêtre, joli, craindre, davantage, partout, soutenir, rue, devoir (n.), à travers, inutile, entourer, peur, cacher, oeuvre, triste, éviter, voiture, fer, parfois, coin, quant à, aussitôt, **agir**.

There are many meanings and special usages hidden in this list of words. But counting only simple or primary meanings, about 45 per cent of the difficulties left in the passages given above to illustrate the importance of the inflected forms disappears. Out of a total of about 720 running words, all but 56 are included above, and among these 56 are such items as *astre, cassette, écurie, friandise, oie, litière,* etc., which would hardly count in any reading knowledge as conventionally defined.

A PLAN FOR TEACHING HOW TO READ

IDIOMATIC PHRASES

In the above passages there is an unusually small proportion of phrases that must be learned as wholes. The following is a list of most of them: *en rapport à; un mouvement d'ensemble; par exemple; du côté de; c'est-à-dire; en effet; tous les jours; non plus; au courant d'une année; à partir de; suivre de peu de temps; de la façon suivante; au contraire; une maîtresse de maison; un remède à nos maux; toute une année; trois fois par jour; à jeun; ce disant; l'homme aux cent yeux; veiller à ce que.*

Most of these phrases contain prepositions and they cease to be difficult or idiomatic if prepositions are considered for what they are, i.e., *functional* words without fixed English equivalents. Real idiomatic difficulties usually involve variations from primary meanings in special contexts. These variations, which constitute separate semantic items in an adequate frequency count, can be illustrated in phrases. If a student practices on a series such as the following, he should have no difficulty in knowing when to take *non* and *plus* separately and when together.

J'en ai *plus* que vous	I have *more* than you
Il n'y en a *plus*	There isn't (aren't) any *more*
Il est *plus grand* que vous	He is *taller* than you
Il n'est *plus* ici	He is *no longer* here
Je n'en ai pas, *non plus*	I haven't any *either*

GRAMMAR

The grammatical knowledge necessary for learning how to read such foreign languages as French or Spanish is extremely small in amount. The information that usually appears under this heading can be listed generally under

(1) word order, (2) equivalent phrases, and (3) pattern phrases. Some examples are as follows:

1. Word order:

    un homme fort, a strong man; *peut-être est-il venu,* perhaps he has come; *je ne le lui ai pas donné,* I have not given it to him; etc.

2. Equivalents:

    *est-il=est-ce qu'il est=*is he? *ai-je=est-ce que j'ai=*have I,= am I having=do I have; *le garçon, a-t-il le livre=* the boy, has he the book=does the boy have the book; *le livre du garçon=*the book of the boy=the boy's book, etc.

3. Pattern phrases:

    le président Roosevelt, President Roosevelt; *il est soldat,* he is a soldier; *il y est allé,* he has gone there; *depuis que je suis ici,* since I have been here; *beaucoup de pain,* much (a great deal) of bread; *les chevaux sont des animaux,* horses are animals, etc.

The problem here is to discover what method of presentation of this material is most economical of effort. In some cases an illustration would probably be sufficient, in others a grammatical statement would be helpful. In any case, the main problem is always memorizing: information about the structure of the language can be reduced to a small compass.

The burden of this plan for teaching how to read is to eliminate, first of all, the confusions due to trying to combine the various aims of reading, speaking, and writing. When the first aim is isolated, a vast number of difficulties that delay progress in this single aim disappear. For recognition knowledge, the prefixes and suffixes can be con-

A PLAN FOR TEACHING HOW TO READ

sidered as units recognizable easily whenever they occur, but for speaking each case must be known separately since these prefixes and suffixes are applicable to some words and not to others (e.g., *im*probable, but not *im*-likely). In reading, the meaning of many idioms, especially those involving prepositions, can be guessed; in speaking, *inference* is of no use at all. Cognates offer almost no difficulty in reading; in speech, each must be known separately, since the tendency of foreigners in speaking is to assume that cognates exist when they do not. And so on.

The problem of the teacher, method-maker, or textbook writer becomes definite. It is the problem of how best to present a definite list of material for memorizing. The relative value of the different ways of handling this material is subject to quantitative measurement and can be determined, therefore, experimentally.

NOTES

BIBLIOGRAPHY

INDEX

NOTES

Chapter I

1. See O. Jespersen, *Language*, p. 146.
2. *Ibid.*, p. 253.
3. Quoted in *Current Opinion*, LXV, 311.
4. C. W. Super, in *Education*, XXXVIII, 42.
5. C. W. Super, in *Popular Science Monthly*, LXXVII, 561.
6. In *Education*, XLV, 277.

Chapter II

1. Quoted in H. Delacroix, *Le langage et la pensée*, p. 274.
2. See *Conférence internationale sur le bilinguisme et l'éducation*, p. 90.
3. E. Zeller, *Language and Thought*, p. 23.
4. Quoted in *Conférence internationale sur le bilinguisme et l'éducation*, p. 91.
5. A. Dauzat, *La philosophie du langage*, p. 43.
6. Quoted in E. Zeller, *Language and Thought*, p. 26.
7. See M. West, *Language in Education*, p. 15.
8. D. J. Saer, "The Effect of Bilingualism on Intelligence," *British Journal of Psychology*, XIV, 24.
9. *Conférence internationale sur le bilinguisme et l'éducation*, p. 90.
10. *Ibid.*, p. 88.
11. *Ibid.*, p. 144.
12. I. Epstein, *La pensée et la polyglossie*, p. 87.

13. O. C. Skelton, *The Language Issue in Canada*, Bulletin Queen's University, 1917.
14. See I. Epstein, *La pensée et la polyglossie*, p. 87.
15. *Conférence internationale sur le bilinguisme et l'éducation*, p. 47.

Chapter III

1. I. Epstein, *Le pensée et la polyglossie*, p. 140.
2. Charles Mercier, in *School and Society*, VIII, 351.
3. C. F. Adams, quoted in *American Mercury*, XIX, 438.
4. K. A. Serafian, in *School and Society*, XXXVII, 621.
5. Professor W. R. Price, in *School and Society*, XXIII, 51, cites the following examples of students' translations: *des oeufs de canards sauvages*, "the eggs of Canadian savages," "ears of wild corn," "beef of dog sausages," "some savage looking horns of oxen," "eggs with hard shells," "bulls with savage horns," etc.

    An example of my own is the following: *Elle buvait à plat ventre l'eau des mares*, "she drank mare's milk on an empty stomach."
6. See also A. Livingston, in *School and Society*, IX, 221.
7. *Ibid.*, p. 221.
8. C. H. Handschin, *Methods of Teaching Modern Languages*, pp. 48 ff.
9. I. Epstein, *La pensée et la polyglossie*, p. 144.
10. E. A. Kirkpatrick, in *School and Society*, XXIII, 814.
11. *Ibid.*, p. 814.

Chapter V

1. C. Sigwalt, *De l'enseignement des langues vivantes*, p. 53.
2. C. F. Sparkman, in *Education*, LIII, 365.
3. See C. Sigwalt, *De l'enseignement des langues vivantes*, p. 28.
4. C. Marcel, *Study of Languages* (New York, Appleton, 1869), p. 203.

5. Example cited by H. Sweet, *The Practical Study of Languages,* p. 74.
6. The example is Kittson's, cited by M. West, in *Bilingualism.*
7. H. R. Huse, *The Psychology of Foreign Language Study* (Chapel Hill, the University of North Carolina Press, 1931), pp. 193 ff.

CHAPTER VI

1. For these and other examples see H. E. Palmer, *The Scientific Study and Teaching of Languages,* pp. 37 ff.
2. See I. Epstein, *La pensée et la polyglossie,* p. 98.
3. H. E. Palmer, *The Scientific Study and Teaching of Languages,* p. 35.
4. M. West, E. Swenson, and others, *A Critical Examination of Basic English,* p. 18.
5. H. E. Palmer, *The Scientific Study and Teaching of Languages,* pp. 37 ff.
6. O. Jespersen, *Language,* p. 217.
7. H. E. Palmer, *The Scientific Study and Teaching of Languages,* pp. 37 ff.
8. Sweet, quoted by O. Jespersen, in *Language,* p. 422.
9. M. West, *Language in Education,* p. 65.

CHAPTER VII

1. M. West, *Language in Education,* p. 135.
2. H. G. Wells, *Mankind in the Making* (New York, Scribner, 1904), p. 322.

SELECTED BIBLIOGRAPHY

Atkins, H. G., and Hutton, H. L. *The Teaching of Modern Foreign Languages in School and University.* London, Arnold, 1920.
Bloomfield, L. *An Introduction to the Study of Language.* New York, Holt, 1914.
Boldyreff, Tatiana W. *By Word of Mouth.* Boston, Gorham Press, 1931.
Brunot, F. *La pensée et la langue.* Paris, Masson, 1922.
Cénac, M. de. *Certains langages créés par des aliénés.* Paris, Jouve.
Colbeck, C. *On the Teaching of Modern Languages.* Cambridge, 1887.
Conférence internationale sur le bilinguisme et l'éducation. Genève, Bureau International d'Education, 1928.
Coulter, V. C. *Readings in Language and Literature.* Ronald Press.
Cummings, T. F. *How to Learn a Language.* New York, 1916.
Dauzat, A. *La philosophie du langage.* Paris, Flamarion, 1917.
Delacroix, H. *Le langage et la pensée.* Paris, Colin, 1924.
———, and others. *La Psychologie du langage.* Paris, Alcan, 1933.
Epstein, I. *La pensée et la polyglossie.* Lausanne, Payot, no date.
Findley, J. J. *Modern Language Learning.* London, Gregg Publishing Co., 1928.
Fouret, L-A. *Les Humanités modernes.* Paris, Didier, 1928.

SELECTED BIBLIOGRAPHY 125

Handschin, C. H. *Methods of Teaching Modern Languages.* New York, World Book Co., 1923.

Jespersen, O. *Language.* London, Geo. Allen and Unwin, 1922.

———, *How to Teach a Foreign Language.* London, Geo. Allen and Unwin, 1904.

Laurie, S. S. *Lectures on Language and Linguistic Method in the School.* Cambridge University Press, 1890.

Leroy, E-B. *Le Langage.* Paris, Alcan, 1905.

Markey, J. F. *The Symbolic Process and Its Integration in Children.* Harcourt, Brace, New York, 1928.

Mead, G. H. *Mind, Self, and Society.* Ed. C. W. Morris. 3 vols. Chicago, University of Chicago Press, 1934.

Palmer, H. E. *The Scientific Study and Teaching of Languages.* London, Harrap, 1917.

Ravizza, Filippo. *Psicologia della lingua.* Torino, 1905.

Sapir, E. *Language.* New York, Harcourt, Brace, 1921.

Saussure, F. de. *Cours de linguistique générale.* Paris, Payot, 1922.

Schweitzer, C., and Simonnot, E. *Méthodologie des langues vivantes.* Paris, Colin, 1921.

Sigwalt, Ch. *De l'enseignement des langues vivantes.* Paris, Colin, 1921.

Sissons, C. B. *Bilingual Schools in Canada.* London, Dent, 1917.

Sweet, H. *The Practical Study of Languages.* New York, Holt, 1900.

West, M. *Bilingualism.* Calcutta, Bureau of Education, Occasional Reports, No. 13, 1926.

———, *Language in Education.* Calcutta, Longmans, Green, 1929.

———, Swenson, E., and others. *A Critical Examination of Basic English.* Toronto, University of Toronto Press, 1934.

Zeller, E. *Language and Thought.* Cleveland, Western Reserve University, 1884.

INDEX

Adams, C. F., 122
Aims of language study, 35, 83
Association. *See* Logical association
ASTP program, v
Atkins, H. G., 124
Automatic speech, 4, 75

Berlitz schools, 38, 69
Bilingualism, 14 ff.
Bloomfield, L., 124
Boldyreff, T. W., 124
Bronner, A. F., 4
Brunot, F., 124

Cénac, M. de, 124
Character, and language, 19; of languages, 46
Cognates, 117
Colbeck, C., 124
Coleman, A., 67
Commercialism, 96
Compromise methods, 82
Conférence international sur le bilinguisme, 121, 122, 124
Coppée, F., 36
Cultural influences, 19
Culture, as an aim, 41
Cummings, T. F., 124

Dauzat, A., 121, 124
Defense of foreign language study, 45 ff.
Definitions, 87
Delacroix, H., 121, 124

Direct methods, 63 ff., 82
Disorganization, 34
Distribution of linguistic talent, 4

Economics, 57
Elementary language study, 46
Emotional instability, 20
English literature, 49-51
Epstein, I., 21, 121, 122, 123, 124
Equivalents, 116
Exercises, 79
Experience and language, 12
Experimentation, 67, 98
Experiments with methods, 65
Extroverts, 12

Facility in speech, 3 ff.
Findley, J. J., 124
Foreign homes, 15; writers, 11
Formal study, 30
Fouret, L.-A., 124
Frequency lists, 92

Governesses, 16
Grammar, 73, 115
Grammar methods, 63, 70 ff., 82
Grouping of words, 113

Handschin, C. H., 122, 125
Henmon, V., 67
Henss, 21
History, 54
Hughes, J., 21
Hutton, H. L., 124

INDEX 127

Idioms, 72, 115
Immaturity and linguistic ability, 6 ff.; of students, 30
Inflected forms, 103 ff.
Inhibition, 20
Interest, 28, 80 ff.
Interference, 10, 24, 25
Introverts, 12
Irregular verbs, 81

Jespersen, O., 121, 123, 125

Kirkpatrick, E. A., 38, 122
Kittson, E. C., 123

Laurie, S. S., 125
Leroy, E-B., 125
Linguistic age, 12
Linguistic units, 71
Literature, 51 ff.
Living speech, 64
Livingston, A., 35, 122
Logical association, 113
Lowell, J. R., 12
Luxemburg, 19

Mackensie, 67
Marcel, C., 122
Markey, J. F., 125
Mead, G. H., 125
Meanings, 84 ff.
Memory, 47, 80, 98, 99
Mental age, 8, 12; development, 21 ff.; discipline, 47
Mercier, C., 32, 122
Methods, 63 ff.
Middletown, 57
Miologs, 84, 93
Monologs, 84
Mother tongue, 20, 48

Natural method, 63, 65
Nieuwenhuis, 17, 21

Oral methods, 67 ff.
Order of words, 116
Organization of material, 104
Over-learning, 26

Palmer, H. E., 84, 86, 123, 125
Paradigms, 79
Passive knowledge, 23; learning, 28, 80
Pattern phrases, 116
Polyglottism, 22
Polylogs, 87
Practical values, 29
Prefixes, 84
Prepositions, 105, 106, 115
Price, W. R., 122
Publishing business, 96
Punctuation, 24

Range of linguistic ability, 11
Ravizza, F., 125
Reading knowledge, 23, 26 ff., 40, 67, 103
Realia, 68
Reflexes, 10, 39
Requirements, 83
Rules, 72, 78

Saer, D. H., 21, 121
Sapir, E., 125
Schools of Education, 98
Science, 55
Semantic variations, 93
Sentences for translation, 76
Serafian, K. A., 122
Sigwalt, Ch., 122, 125
Simmonot, E., 125
Sissons, C. B., 125
Skelton, O. C., 122
Smith, F., 21, 24
Social science, 52 ff.
Sound association, 113
Speaking knowledge, 3 ff., 23, 26 ff.
Spelling, 24
Spoken language, 64, 65
Stern, W., 17
Studial learning, 77
Suffixes, 84
Suggestion, 52, 80
Super, C. W., 121
Sweet, H., 123, 125
Sweitzer, C., 125

Swensen, E., 123
Swift, J., 3

Teacher problem, 99
Textbooks, 66, 81, 83, 89, 95 ff.
Thorndike, E. L., 85
Thought and language, 23
Translation, 49, 74 ff.
Type phrases, 91
Typographical devices, 94

Units of expression 76 ff., 84 ff.

Vander Beke, G. E., 86
Veblen, T., 57

Verbalism, 31
Verb forms, 104, 105
Verheyren, 22
Vocabulary, 112 ff.

Wales, 18, 21
Wells, H. G., 98, 123
West, M., 21, 23, 83, 88, 121, 123, 125
Word counts, 84 ff.; lists, 79; order, 116
Worrel, W. H., 6

Zeller, E., 18, 121, 125

www.ingramcontent.com/pod-product-compliance
Lightning Source LLC
Chambersburg PA
CBHW030116010526
44116CB00005B/274